Principles of
Macro
Economics

Neil Fuller BSc (Econ), MSc, MCIPS

Revisions by
Nigel Proctor BA, MA (Econ), PGCE

TUDOR

Published in Great Britain by Tudor Business Publishing Ltd.

First published 1987
Reprinted with revisions 1990, 1993

Second edition 1997

British Library Cataloguing in Publication Data:
A catalogue record for this book is available from the British Library

ISBN   1–872807–62–3

Cover design by T/S Graphics

Typeset in 10/12 pt Palatino by GreenGate Publishing Services, Tonbridge, Kent
Printed in Great Britain by the Athenaeum Press, Gateshead, Tyne & Wear

Contents

Introduction

For the new edition of this book it was felt that a more radical revision than usual was required. Hence not only has all the data and background information been up-dated but the entire text has been brought up-to-date to meet the needs of today's readers.

As with the earlier editions, the book is intended to assist students who have little or no prior knowledge of macro economics to rapidly grasp the main principles of the subject. It covers the requirements of most courses including A level, the first year of degree courses, the foundation stages of the professional bodies, graduate conversion courses, and should be particularly suitable for those on single semesters in macro economics. It has proved especially suitable for those students with no knowledge of the subject who need to proceed rapidly to a high level of understanding.

Theoretical aspects of macro economics are covered in detail and are illustrated with actual data wherever possible in order to link the theoretical and applied aspects of the subject. It is essential however that students recognise the need to read widely in the press, journals, and other published sources in order to keep abreast of events in this ever -changing area of study. Chapter 19 provides an up-to-date assessment of the major trends in the UK economy at the time of writing.

In order to aid their learning of the subject students are recommended to read through a chapter of the book and then test their understanding by attempting the end-of-chapter self -assessment questions, all of which can be answered from the material contained within the chapter.

The approach taken in the book is intended to clarify the key issues involved. Where mathematical proofs are involved they have been put into appendices in order to avoid confusing the less mathematical reader.

Material on the single European market and single currency has been included in order to incorporate the growing importance of the European dimension to the UK economy. The chapter on development economics reflects the growing interest in this area of study.

A glossary of terms has been included in order to provide an easy source of reference to the terminology of economics which those new to the subject often find difficult to grasp.

I am grateful for the help given to me by Nigel Proctor both in restructuring the material and for his assistance in up-dating the contents. I would also like to acknowledge Richard Ledward of Staffordshire University for his advice and assistance with the data collection, and my colleague David Barnes for his assistance and comments.

Neil Fuller 1997

1

National income

1 National product

National income refers to the aggregate, or total, income of the nation which results from economic activity. Income however depends upon how much output is produced and as output is a continuous process rather than a stock, we have to measure this output over a specified time period, usually one year. Total output is referred to as **national product,** and includes all the **goods** and **services** produced each year.

2 A definition

National income was defined by Alfred Marshall as 'the aggregate net product of and sole source of payment to, all the agents of production.' If this definition is studied closely we can identify three components:

- Aggregate net product of, i.e. total output.
- Sole source of payment, i.e. incomes.
- All the agents of production, i.e. how the national product is distributed, and therefore the source of all expenditure.

3 Measurement of national income

From this definition we can identify three possible methods of measurement:

- **output**
- **income**
- **expenditure.**

Measurement by either of these methods will produce identical results because theoretically:

national income = national output = national expenditure

4 Circular flow

In order to understand the concept of income as a **flow** it is useful to study the **circular flow of income** in the form of a **flow diagram**. If Figure 1.1 is studied closely it can be seen that households provide the supply of productive services to firms and in return receive the factor rewards of wages, rent, interest and profit. These are the total of all incomes to households and will therefore form the basis of all expenditures. When expenditures are made with firms in the form of consumption then there must be an equivalent flow of goods and services from firms to households. It is therefore possible to measure each of these flows and achieve the same result, hence the conclusion that national income = national output = national expenditure. In reality the circular flow Figure 1.1 needs to be highly qualified, for example much of national expenditure is in the form of investment expenditure between firms, however it does illustrate the concept of national income as a flow.

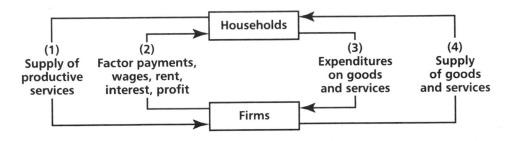

Figure 1.1

5 A summary

To summarise therefore national income can be regarded as:

- **the total value of the goods and services produced by all the industries and public services during the year.**
- **the total expenditure on final goods and services for consumption and investment purposes during the year.**
- **the factor cost of national output in terms of all the earnings in producing the national output.**

6 Real values

National income is estimated in money terms because money is the most convenient 'measuring rod', however care must be taken in comparing national income over time as a rise in the monetary value of national income does not necessarily imply a rise in living standards. The only real measure of whether national income has grown is whether the **real** value of output has increased, and it is possible that any apparent increase is a result of rising prices. For this reason data must be 'deflated' by a suitable index before comparisons of national income between different time periods can be made. One method of deflating data is to use the retail price index.

$$\frac{\text{national income at current prices}}{\text{RPI}} \times 100$$

This method produces national income at **constant prices**. If the index was based on prices in 1995, i.e. 1995 = 100 then the index could be said to be 'at 1995 prices'. As inflation has been removed from the data comparisons over time become more meaningful. National income and expenditure (The Blue Book) presents national income data in both current and constant prices. (See Chapter 9, Appendix for example).

7 GNP and GDP

Gross **National** Product **(GNP)** and Gross **Domestic** Product **(GDP)** differ because some output produced within the UK is produced by foreign owned firms and the profits and interest are paid abroad to the owners. Similarly some productive resources overseas are owned by UK residents and the profits and interest are remitted back to them. The difference between payments made abroad and payments received from abroad is referred to as **net property income from abroad** and constitutes the difference between GNP and GDP. Gross domestic product as the name suggests, refers to the output of all domestically (i.e. UK) **located** resources, whilst GNP is the output of all resources **owned** by UK residents, i.e:

Gross National Product = Gross Domestic Product + net property income from abroad

N.B. domestic product is output produced within the UK.

8 Capital consumption

During the course of production assets become worn out and require replacement. This is referred to as **capital consumption** or more commonly, **depreciation**. This is a cost which must be incorporated within national income accounting and is deducted from gross national product to obtain the **net national product**; also referred to as the **national income**, i.e.

Gross National Product less depreciation = Net National Product = National Income

We can now consider the three methods of estimation separately.

9 The expenditure method

This method measures the total amount of final expenditures in the course of a year. It includes:

- Consumer's expenditure on goods and services.
- Investment expenditure by firms.
- Additions to stocks are included as nominal expenditure.
- Expenditure by public authorities on goods and services.

A number of adjustments must be made to the data in order to arrive at the final figure:

- Because the data collected is at market prices a number of adjustments have to be made in order to find the factor cost, i.e. market prices may be distorted by taxes and subsidies, and may not reflect the true cost. As subsidies artificially reduce the market price they are added back on, and as indirect taxes raise the price they are deducted, i.e.

Factor cost = market price + subsidies – indirect taxes

- An adjustment has to be made for the sale of output abroad (exports) and the purchase of goods from abroad (imports).

The expenditure method of calculation is therefore as shown in Table 1.1.

TABLE 1.1	The expenditure method
	Consumers' expenditure
Plus	Public authorities current expenditure on goods and services
Plus	Gross capital formation (investment) at home including increases in stocks
=	Total domestic expenditure at market prices
Plus	Exports and income from abroad
Less	Imports and Income paid abroad
Less	Taxes on expenditure
Plus	Subsidies
=	Gross national product at factor cost
Less	Capital consumption (depreciation)
=	National income

10 The output method

This method measures the total output of all consumer goods and services, and investment goods, produced by all the firms in the country during the year. This measure can be obtained by totalling the **final** goods and services produced, or by taking the totals of **value added.** For example, imagine a firm which mines nitrates and sells the crude product to a chemical extracting company at £80 per ton. After refining it is sold to a fertiliser company at £100 per ton who produce and package garden fertiliser for sale to the retail trade at £150 per ton. The retailer sells it to his retail customers at the equivalent of £250 per ton. This is represented diagramatically in Figure 1.2.

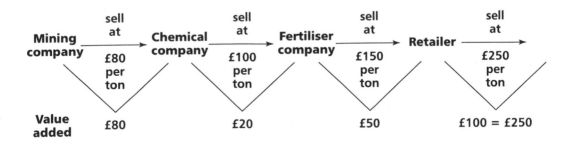

Figure 1.2

It should be noted that the sum of the value added (£250) is the same as the value of retail sales. Therefore either the value of the final goods or the total of value added can be used. What cannot be done is to add the value of output at each stage because this would involve counting the same item more than once, i.e. the £100 to the fertiliser manufacturer includes the £80 to the mining company. This error is referred to as **double counting** and can be a serious source of error in national income accounting.

The output of all industry is classified according to the official Standard Industrial Classification (SIC) and is added together to obtain total output.

A number of 'adjustments' have to be made to the output figures:

- Artificial increases in stock values due to inflation (stock appreciation) have to be deducted.
- Net property income from abroad.
- The 'residual error' (statistical discrepancy).

TABLE 1.2 The output method	
	Agriculture, forestry and fishing
Plus	Mining and quarrying
Plus	Manufacturing
Plus	Construction
Plus	Gas, electricity and water
Plus	Transport
Plus	Communication
Plus	Distributive trades
Plus	Insurance, banking and finance
Plus	Public administration and defence
Plus	Public health and educational services
Plus	Other services
Plus	Ownership of dwellings
	Total domestic output
Less	Stock appreciation
Plus/Minus	Residual error
Plus/Minus	Net property income from abroad
=	Gross national product at factor cost
Less	Capital consumption
=	National income

11 The income method

- This method measures the total money value of all incomes received by persons and firms in the country during the year. These incomes may be in the form of wages, salaries, rent or profit.
- Care must be taken to exclude **transfer payments** such as student grants, pensions and unemployment benefit. These are excluded because they do not represent payment for a contribution to output but are transfers of income from one group to another.
- Adjustments have to be made for the undistributed profits of companies and the surpluses of the nationalised industries which are paid to the government.
- Adjustments also have to be made for stock appreciation and net property income from abroad.

The income method of calculation is therefore:

TABLE 1.3 The income method	
	Income from employment
Plus	Income from self employment
Plus	Profits of private companies and public enterprises
Plus	Rent
=	Total domestic income
Less	Stock appreciation
Plus/Minus	Residual error
Plus/Minus	Net property income from abroad
=	Gross national product
Less	Capital consumption (depreciation)
=	**National income**

In theory the three methods must balance, but in reality they may differ due to errors and delays in returns; the residual error is added to ensure that they do balance. The source of some of these errors is found later and the figures are adjusted in subsequent years.

12 Problems of calculation

A number of problems are encountered in the calculation of national income, the main ones being:

- The problem of double counting (see 10).
- Transfer payments (see 11).
- Underestimates may occur where goods and services do not enter the market and are therefore unrecorded. For example, goods consumed by those producing them, as is the case with farmers; or farm labourers who receive part of their income in kind.

- Unpaid personal services are excluded, e.g. the work of housewives. Housework is an indirect contribution to output in that it enables others in the family to make a more direct contribution.
- Data collection may be inadequate due to firms failing to send in returns or making errors. Also much of the information is originally collected for different purposes, e.g. tax returns.
- The growth of the 'black economy'; in recent years it has been suggested that as much as 7½% of GDP may go unrecorded. The 'black economy' refers to that part of economic activity which is undeclared and therefore unrecorded for tax purposes, and is therefore deemed to be 'illegal'. Research suggests that there has been considerable growth in this sector over recent years.

13 International comparisons

International comparisons of national income as a basis for comparing 'standards of living' is subject to a number of qualifications:

- Whether or not a particular level of national income implies a high material standard of living also depends upon population size, and measurement requires an estimate of **per capita** income, i.e.

$$\text{NNP at factor cost} = \frac{\textbf{Per capita income}}{\textbf{Population}}$$

Therefore the growth of NNP must be greater than population growth in order for living standards to rise.
- 'Standard of living' is a subjective evaluation and other nations may put more value upon non-material aspects which do not enter national income accounting.
- Climatic differences may mean that although national income may be lower in some countries they have to spend less on fuel and clothing to keep warm.
- Transport in large countries where there are dispersed centres of population may absorb a higher proportion of national income.
- The use of exchange rates to convert national income statistics into a common currency unit may produce unreliable results for comparison purposes.

14 Living standards

Whether or not an increase in national income is the same thing as an increase in welfare is a matter of some discussion as national income measurements fail to include factors which many would suggest were an essential aspect of 'welfare', but which cannot be measured purely in terms of material goods. In particular they would indicate:

- 'Externalities' such as environmental pollution which may actually become worse as the rate of growth of national income increases.
- The level of provision of 'merit' goods such as education, health and welfare.
- The production of 'demerit' goods such as alcohol and tobacco.
- The level of provision of government transfers such as pensions, grants and social security benefits which are specifically excluded from the statistics in order to avoid double counting, but it could be argued that they cannot be omitted from any measure of welfare.

National income measurements do provide however an indication of whether or not output, and therefore incomes, is rising, and provided the qualifications are borne in mind during interpretation they do provide a useful indication of the trends in the economy.

The following page shows national income statistics for the UK 1995 measured by each of the three methods.

Self assessment questions

1 What is meant by the circular flow of income?

2 State the three methods by which national income can be calculated.

3 How does the problem of 'double counting' occur?

4 What are 'transfer payments'?

5 Outline the problems which occur in making international comparisons of national income.

6 Describe in detail one method of national income calculation.

TABLE 1.4	
UK National Income 1995 (millions £)	
Income	
Income from employment	377,900
Income from self employment	67,700
Gross trading profits of companies	91,000
Gross trading surplus of public corporations	4,600
Gross trading surplus of general government enterprises	600
Rent	62,800
Imputed charge for consumption of non trading capital	4,700
Total domestic income	609,300
Less stock appreciation	−4,800
Residual error	−200
Gross domestic product at factor cost	604,300
Net property income from abroad	9,600
Gross national product	613,900
Less capital consumption	73,300
National income (net national product)	540,600

(Continued)	
Output	
Agriculture, forestry and fishing	11,900
Mining, quarrying, including oil and gas extraction	14,600
Energy and water supply	15,800
Manufacturing	131,700
Construction	31,800
Wholesale and retail trade, repairs, hotels and restaurants	84,700
Transport, storage and communications	50,800
Financial intermediation, red estate, renting and business activities	158,200
Public administration, defence, social security	39,500
Education, health and social work	73,000
Other services	23,200
Adjustment for financial services	−30,700
Statistical discrepancy	<u>−200</u>
Gross domestic product at factor cost	<u>604,300</u>
Net property income from abroad	9,600
Gross national product at factor cost	<u>613,900</u>
Less capital consumption	73,300
National income (net national product)	540,600

(Continued)	
Expenditure	
Customers expenditure	447,200
General government final consumption	149,500
Gross domestic fixed capital	105,400
Value of physical increase in stock and work in progress	3,900
Total domestic expenditure	706,000
Exports of goods and services	197,600
Total final expenditure	903,600
Less imports of goods and services	−203,100
Statistical discrepancy	400
Gross domestic product at market prices	700,900
Net property income from abroad	9,600
Gross national product at market prices	710,500
Less taxes on expenditure	−103,600
Subsidies	7,000
Gross national product at factor cost	613,900
Less capital consumption	73,300
National income (net national product)	540,600

2

International trade

1 Reasons for trade

Nations engage in international trade for a variety of reasons:

- Due to **climatic differences** some goods would not be available in many parts of the world without trade. For example, coffee grows prolifically between the tropics, but not elsewhere. This is true of many natural commodities.
- **Natural resources** are not evenly distributed throughout the world, for example many countries have no coal or oil reserves whilst others have a surplus over their domestic requirements.
- **Skills and technology** are also not distributed evenly and whilst some countries have a high level of technological development others have a much lower level, both will therefore tend to produce goods of a different nature.
- Because factors of production and natural resources tend to be **immobile** it is more convenient to specialise in the production of those goods in which there is a natural, or acquired advantage, and trade the surplus not required for domestic consumption for those goods which cannot be produced.

2 Specialisation and trade

Although it was stated above that certain crops would not grow naturally in some regions of the world, it is not true that they could not be grown given sufficient diversion of resources to their production. For example, bananas can be grown quite successfully in heated greenhouses in the UK, but the cost would be very high and therefore the output would only be available to the wealthiest people. It is far more efficient for each country to use its resources in the production of those goods in which they have a cost advantage and trade with other nations to obtain those goods which are not produced. For example, the UK has an advantage over the West Indies in the production of machinery whilst the West Indies for climatic reasons can grow an abundance of bananas. It is therefore more efficient for Britain to **specialise** in the production of machines and trade with the West Indies for bananas. Both countries then enjoy the **gains from trade** which result from **specialisation**.

Specialisation and trade increase world output and enables everybody to enjoy a higher standard of living than would be otherwise available. A wider variety of goods are made available to more people.

3 The law of comparative advantage

The **law of comparative costs** shows that countries can gain from specialisation and trade provided that there is some difference in the **relative costs** of producing those goods. The **opportunity cost** of producing a good domestically may be too high, for example the growing of bananas in the UK quoted above.

To illustrate the law of comparative costs, suppose there are two countries X and Y. Both produce just two goods, beef and cars. Both countries have an equivalent amount of capital and labour but X has abundant grasslands and suitable climate for beef production whilst Y has less favourable climate and agricultural conditions but a more highly skilled workforce. There are no unemployed factors in either country. When both countries are using their resources equally to produce both goods output is as follows:

Country	Beef (Units)	Cars (Units)
X	1000	200
Y	200	1000
Total production before specialisation	1200	1200

If however each country specialises in the production of those goods at which they are most efficient, i.e. X specialises in beef and Y in cars, then output is as follows:

Country	Beef (Units)	Cars (Units)
X	2000	NIL
Y	NIL	2000
Total production after specialisation	2000	2000

(Note: It was originally assumed that each country was using half of its resources in the production of each good, therefore if country X could produce 1000 units with half its resources logically it could produce 2000 with all its resources.)

The **net gains** from specialisation are 800 units of beef and 800 units of cars (note: in specialising X gave up the production of 200 cars and Y the production of 200 beef units leaving a **net** gain of 800 of each). In this example each country specialised in the production of goods in which they had a **comparative advantage.**

4 The principle of absolute advantage

If one country is more efficient in the production of both goods, i.e. has an **absolute advantage** then it may still be worthwhile engaging in trade if one country specialises in the production of those goods in which its disadvantage is least; referred to as **least comparative disadvantage,** and the other country those goods in which the **comparative advantage is greatest.**

Suppose that country X was more efficient in the production of both beef and cars, and the positions before specialisation are as follows:

Country	Beef (Units)	Cars (Units)
X	1000	600
Y	900	200
Total production before specialisation	1900	800

Specialisation is still worthwhile as X's comparative advantage is greatest in car production, i.e. three times as efficient whereas X is only 1.1 times more efficient in production of beef. Therefore if X specialises in cars and devotes nine-tenths of its resources to car production and one tenth to beef production, whilst Y specialises in beef, total production will be as follows:

Country	Beef (Units)	Cars (Units)
X	200	1080
Y	1800	NIL
Total production after specialisation	2000	1080
Gain	100	280

5 Gains from trade

Using the same example the **gains from trade** can be illustrated by the use of production possibility curves (or boundaries) as in Figure 2.1. The production possibility boundaries are linear because it is assumed the diminishing returns do not occur as resources are transferred from one use to another. In the figure the lines Y–Y and X–X are the production possibility boundaries of both countries prior to specialisation and trade. The line T–T is the total production possibility boundary for both countries after specialisation and prior to trade. Although specialisation has brought gains in total production trade must occur. The **terms of trade**, i.e. beef: cars, must lie between the two sets of (internal) domestic opportunity cost ratios which are:

In X 1.6 : 1 (beef : cars)
    Y 4.5 : 1 (beef : cars)

Hence the terms of trade must lie between 1.6 and 4.5: 1, for example 3:1.

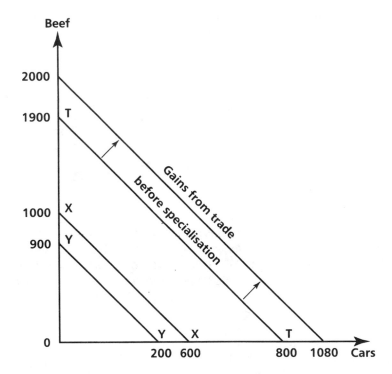

Figure 2.1

If the terms of trade are 3:1, X can trade 1 car with Y and receive 3 units of beef in return, whereas to transfer resources domestically X would only gain 1.6 units of beef. Conversely Y can gain 1 car in exchange for 3 units of beef by trading, whereas to gain 1 car by transferring resources domestically it would give up 4.5 units of beef. Both countries will therefore gain from specialisation and exchange providing the terms of trade lie between the two domestic (non trading) opportunity cost ratios.

Trade will continue as long as the **domestic opportunity cost ratios in the two countries are different**. Trade would cease when it cost more in terms of resources for X to import beef than to produce it. If X could produce beef more cheaply in terms of cars than Y by transferring resources to beef production then trade would cease.

Trade theory must be qualified however to allow for the fact that there may be some loss of efficiency when transferring production from one good to another. Also, transport costs will be incurred, which may outweigh a marginal cost advantage.

6 Terms of trade

The **terms of trade** refer to the rate at which one nation's goods can be exchanged for those of others. In the example above it was 3:1. In reality physical goods are not exchanged but prices are paid in various currencies. The terms of trade are measured by means of a **terms of trade index** which is calculated as:

$$\frac{\text{index of export prices}}{\text{index of import prices}} \times 100$$

The base year of the index is 100. An improvement in the terms of trade is said to be **favourable** and shows as an increase in the index, indicating that a given volume of exports can be exchanged for a greater volume of imports. A fall in the index is said to be **unfavourable** as a given volume of exports can only be exchanged for a smaller volume of imports. The terms of trade index has important implications for the UK's performance as a trading nation.

Table 2.1 shows the UK terms of trade 1981–1995.

TABLE 2.1	
YEAR	TERMS OF TRADE (1990=100)
1981	105.9
1982	104.3
1983	102.6
1984	101.5
1985	101.9
1986	96.1
1987	96.7
1988	98.6
1989	98.8
1990	100
1991	100.2
1992	101.4
1993	103.5
1994	102.2
1995	98.9

Source: Economic Trends

7 Trade restrictions

Despite the gains from free international trade, nations have frequently attempted to restrict the amount of trade in order to protect their domestic economies from the effects of foreign competition. The competition may be from lower cost producers due to either, or both, greater efficiency and lower wage costs. Such an attitude is referred to as 'protectionism' and restrictions on trade may take a variety of forms:

- Tariffs – taxes on imports, generally referred to as duties.
- Quotas – physical limits on the quantities of specified goods which can be imported.
- Subsidies – to domestic producers to reduce their prices below those of foreign competitors.
- Exchange control regulations – limit the amount of foreign currency available to pay for imports.
- Physical controls – a complete ban or embargo.

8 Arguments for trade restrictions

The arguments generally put forward in favour of restrictions on trade are:

- To protect a new or developing industry – the 'infant industry case'.
- To assist in the elimination of a balance of payments deficit.
- To protect the domestic economy against unemployment caused by too many imported goods.
- To protect strategically important industries such as iron, steel and shipbuilding.
- To protect the domestic economy from 'unfair' competition, in particular 'dumping' where excess production is sold abroad at cost in order to cover marginal costs only, and allow profits to be made on the domestic market; or where 'cheap' labour is being used (e.g. child labour).

9 The costs of protection

Protecting domestic industries from competition in order to ensure their survival is a dubious argument. In the long run protection from competition results in a loss of efficiency and inventiveness, and when eventually industries have to face international competition again they will be weak and ill-equipped to do so.

The costs of protection however are generally borne by consumers who are forced to pay higher prices and have a restricted choice of goods. Also, trade is possibly the best way of forging links between countries and promoting international co-operation. Attempts to interfere with trade generally result in some form of retaliation which may lead to a disastrous trade war where everybody loses.

10 Changes over time

It cannot be assumed that because a country has a comparative advantage in the production of a particular good that it will retain that advantage indefinitely. The centres of comparative advantage in production tend to change over time, particularly with changes in technology and the growth of capital resources, for example, Britain's comparative advantage in the production of cotton textiles has shifted towards the cotton producing countries. Changes in comparative advantage can be a major cause of **structural unemployment** (see Chapter 5).

11 The Single European Market

The creation of a Single European Market **(SEM)** within the European Union (EU) is an example of trade theory in practice. The idea is that all barriers to trade within the community would be removed, resulting in increased trade and output. The creation of the SEM was originally stated as a prime objective of The Treaty of Rome, i.e. a single European trading block which would match the USA, the former USSR, etc. in terms of output, production and population.

Internal tariffs on industrial goals had been largely eliminated by 1977, but numerous obstacles to trade within the European Union remained, and it is these remaining obstacles that the SEM hoped to remove. The objective of a SEM by 1992 was proposed by the head of the European Commission, Jacques Delors, and was formalised in the Commissioner's White Paper 'Completing the Internal Market' (June 1985).

12 Barriers to trade

The main **barriers to trade** and the benefits from liberalisation were identified and quantified by Paolo Cecchini in 'The European Challenge 1992 – The Benefits of a Single Market' published on behalf of the European Commission. Internal tariffs had largely been eliminated by 1977. However, substantial trade obstacles were still in existence.

- **Physical barriers** – in particular frontier delays and administrative burdens imposed on goods on transit.
- **Technical barriers** – inter country differences in technical regulations, standards and differences in business law.
- **Fiscal barriers** – especially differing rates of VAT and excise duties. The 1985 White Paper identified the following further barriers:
  - Restrictions on competition for public sector contracts, which in practice favoured domestic suppliers.
  - Special arrangements for specific industries, eg. the Multifibre Arrangement, adopted by individual countries.
  - The agricultural sector – as a consequence of the Common Agricultural Policy (CAP).

13 The liberalisation programme

The **White Paper's liberalisation programme** consisted of three main components:

- The removal of physical barriers to the movement of goods and people.
- The removal of technical barriers covering quality standards, public procurement and regulation.
- The removal of fiscal barriers, e.g. harmonisation of VAT rates.

14 The Cecchini Report

The Cecchini Report estimated that the liberalisation measures would result in economic gains to the SEM of the following order:

Table 2.2	
Static welfare gains	70bm–190bm ECU's (2.5–6.5% of the EC 1988 GDP)
Increased growth rate	1% p.a
Increased employment	2 million additional jobs
Reduced consumer prices (%GDP)	6%
External balance	1%
Budgetary balance (%GDP)	1%

The Cecchini Report stated that four major economic consequences may be expected from the combined impact of the elimination of barriers and the subsequent boost to competition:

- **Significant reduction in costs**, thanks to improved exploitation by companies of **economies of scale in production** and business organisation;
- **Improved efficiency within companies, widespread industrial reorganisation**, and a situation where **prices move downward** towards production costs under the pressure of more competitive markets;
- New patterns of competition between entire industries and reallocation of resources as, in home market conditions, real comparitive advantages play the determining role in market success;
- **Increased innovation**, new business processes and products generated by the **dynamics of the internal market.**

Eventually the free movement of goods, labour, and capital within the EU should enable the member states to enjoy the gains from the operation of the laws of comparitive advantage. Resources will tend to gravitate towards those areas of production in which they are relatively most efficient, hence member states will specialise in the production of those goods in which they have the greatest comparitive advantage. By having free trade with other member states the whole community will benefit from the increase in output.

15 Conclusions

At present it is impossible to judge just what impact the SEM has had on British industry.

Opportunities exist for the large business but it would seem to have made very little difference to the small and medium sized companies.

The harmonisation of standards and economic indicators such as tax rates has not occurred as envisaged.

One definite result of the SEM has been the increased number of European mergers. There is still much to do before a true SEM actually exists.

Self-assessment questions

1 Distinguish between an absolute and a comparitive advantage.
2 What are the gains from trade?
3 What are the 'terms of trade'?
4 How is the 'terms of trade index' calculated?
5 Why might nations impose restrictions on trade?
6 What are the main arguments against restrictions on trade?
7 What forms may restrictions on trade take?

3

Balance of payments

1 Recording transactions

The balance of payments in the accounting sense is a record of all the transactions of the UK with the rest of the world. Like all accounting balance sheets the balance of payments taken as a whole **must** be in balance; what is more important however is the performance in the component sections.

Table 3.1 illustrates the summary balance of payments accounts for the UK for 1995.

TABLE 3.1	
	£ m
1.Visible balance (trade balance)	-11,550
2.Invisible balance	+4,880
3.CURRENT BALANCE	-6,670
4.Net Transactions in U.K. Assets and Liabilities	+4,798
5.Balancing Item	+1,872
(note (3) + (4) + (5) = NIL)	

The figures shown are net figures, i.e. the figure after imports (inflows) are offset by corresponding exports (outflows).

2 The current balance

The part of the accounts which receives most attention is the **current balance**. The current balance has two components, **visibles** and **invisibles.**

● The **visible balance** comprises of the import and export of **goods**. Until the 1980s Britain rarely had a surplus on visibles, however after the advent of North Sea oil a surplus on visible trade was regularly achieved although by the mid 1980s the trade balance had again deteriorated.

- **Invisibles** refers to trade services and to transfers. These include:
  - Shipping.
  - Civil aviation.
  - Insurance.
  - Banking.
  - Tourism.
  - Interest and profits.
  - Government transfers, e.g. military and diplomatic expenditure.
  - Private transfers.

Britain has generally had a substantial surplus on invisible trade, sufficient to outweigh the deficit on visibles. Although on occasion the deficit on trade has been so great that even after allowing for invisibles there was a substantial **deficit on current account**. Table 3.2 illustrates how a trade deficit can become a current account surplus after the inclusion of invisibles.

TABLE 3.2	
	£m
VISIBLE TRADE	
Exports	2500
Imports	3300
Trade deficit	- 800
INVISIBLE TRADE	
Exports	1900
Imports	1000
Invisible surplus	+ 900
CURRENT ACCOUNT SURPLUS	+ 100

The current account is generally taken as being the main indicator of the nation's performance in international trade.

3 Transactions in UK assets and liabilities

Transactions in UK assets and liabilities refers to the increases or decreases in the UK assets and liabilities during that period. It refers only to new transactions in that period and not the total stock of UK external assets or liabilities. This section therefore records the increase or decrease in the following:

- Foreign assets, including foreign currency held by UK residents and the UK government.
- Liabilities of the UK to the residents of foreign countries. They represent an increase or decrease in the ownership of UK assets which are held by overseas residents which may be individuals, firms, or governments, and include holdings of sterling. In the

presentation of the accounts it is important to note that an increase in the external assets held by UK residents is indicated with a negative (–) value and an increase in external liabilities by a positive (+) value.

A deficit on current account may be offset by a surplus on the capital transactions, i.e. a net asset inflow. This may imply however an increase in future invisible outflows when the remittance of profits and interest overseas has to be made.

Official financing refers to the changes which take place in the reserves if the deficit (or surplus) on the current account is not matched by a surplus (or deficit) on the capital transactions. If, for example, there is an overall deficit then it must have been met either from the official reserves which would have been reduced, or foreign currency borrowing from abroad. A surplus would increase the reserves or be used to repay earlier loans. This is included under the assets section of the accounts.

4 The balancing item

As stated earlier the balance of payments taken as a whole must balance in the accounting sense because every transaction has a double aspect; as in accounting every debit must have a matching credit. For example, if a UK firm sells goods to a foreign firm then the value of the export is a credit (+) in the current account, however the payment for the export represents a debit (–) in the deposits held by the foreign firm in UK banks.

The sum of the current balance and the net transaction balance must therefore be zero. In reality however due to various errors and omissions this may not be the case and the **balancing item** is added to the net transactions balance of the capital account, which is known with a higher degree of certainty, in order to ensure that the account balances. Eventually the source of some of the errors is found and the adjustments to the accounts made later. Concern has been expressed over recent years regarding the size of the balancing item and its implications for the reliability of the accounts.

5 Equilibrium/disequilibrium

Reference to **equilibrium** or **disequilibrium** in the balance of payments usually refers to the **current account**. Equilibrium is generally taken to refer to the fact that exports are equal to imports. This definition has to be qualified however, and before it is truly meaningful should include discussion of:

- The time period involved.
- The exchange rate – if the exchange rate is freely floating then in theory equilibrium in the balance of payments will always be attained in the long run. (See Chapter 4).
- The exchange rate may be managed in order to manipulate transactions in such a way as to make them balance.

6 Balance of payments deficit

A deficit in the balance of payments means that in the short run the nation is enjoying a higher material standard of living than it would otherwise do. Such a situation can however only be maintained for as long as there are adequate reserves. In the absence of bottomless reserves no country can run a balance of payments deficit indefinitely.

7 Policies to correct a deficit

Policies to correct a balance of payments deficit include:

- A reduction in the exchange rate to make exports cheaper and imports dearer.
- Import controls – which may result in 'retaliation'.
- Expenditure 'dampening policies' – reducing the level of domestic demand for all goods including imports. This has high costs in terms of domestic output and therefore employment.
- Expenditure 'switching policies', intended to shift domestic expenditure from imports to domestically produced goods. An example here is raising the price of imports relative to domestic goods by imposing duties.
- Subsidies or aid to exporters.
- Increasing the domestic rate of interest in order to attract capital inflows.

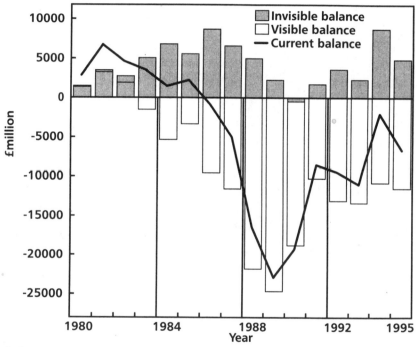

Figure 3.1

8 Recent trends

Figure 3.1 illustrates Britain's balance of payments 1980 to 1995.

Quite clearly there has been an improvement in Britain's current account balance from the large deficits of 1989 and 1990. Economic recovery is part of the reason along with an increase in exports of cars in particular. Many of these are cars produced by foreign owned manufacturers such as Nissan, Toyota and Honda.

At the same time imports have grown and services have under performed compared to Britain's major competitors. The outlook for the rest of the 1990s is therefore not as good as the trend would indicate.

Self assessment questions

1 Distinguish between visibles and invisibles.

2 How is the current balance obtained?

3 Does a deficit on the balance of payments necessarily imply a reduction in the standard of living of the nation?

4 How is the total currency flow obtained?

5 In what ways may a deficit on the balance of payments be financed?

6 Discuss the arguments for and against import controls in the UK.

7 What policies can a government adopt in order to correct a balance of payments deficit?

4

Exchange rates

1 The price of currency

The exchange rate refers to the rate at which one currency can be exchanged for another, e.g. pounds for deutschmarks, or dollars. As we are discussing how many dollars etc. we can obtain for a pound then it is the same as discussing the **price of foreign currency**. In the rest of this discussion reference will be made only to the rate of exchange between dollars and pounds (sterling), there are of course rates of exchange between all currencies and the analysis of them is identical.

Exchange rates are important because they determine the prices at which UK goods will be sold abroad, and the price at which foreign goods will be sold in the UK. They therefore have a direct effect on the balance of payments and the domestic economy.

2 Changes in the value of the pound

If the exchange rate between pounds and dollars was originally £1 = $2, and then on the international market began to be exchanged at £1 = $1.50 we would refer to a **fall** in the **value of the pound** relative to the dollar, and the price of UK goods selling in America in dollar prices would fall. If the rate of exchange became £1 = $2.50 we would refer to a **rise** in the **value of the pound** relative to the dollar and the dollar price of UK goods in America would rise.

3 The determination of exchange rates

As mentioned above, the exchange rate is really the price of foreign currency and as is the case with other goods, price is determined by supply and demand. In the absence of intervention by governments therefore, exchange rates are determined by the demand for, and supply of, currencies. The price of the pound in terms of the dollar will depend upon the demand for the pound by holders of dollars and the supply of pounds will be from holders of pounds who want to buy dollars. The demand for pounds is derived from the demand by overseas residents for British goods and who require pounds to pay for them. The supply of pounds is derived from the demand by UK residents for goods from overseas and who require foreign currency to pay for them. In exchanging pounds for foreign currency, in this case dollars, the supply of pounds is increased. The demand for, and supply of, pounds takes place on the **foreign exchange markets**, and the **equilibrium exchange rate** will be where demand and supply are equal. In Figure 4.1 the equilibrium exchange rate is where the demand and supply for sterling are equal. Clearly the value of a nation's currency depends ultimately upon its overseas trade performance. A balance of payments surplus would therefore indicate a high demand for pounds in order to pay for UK goods, the exchange rate would therefore be high relative to other currencies. A deficit would imply an excess supply of pounds and a weak currency.

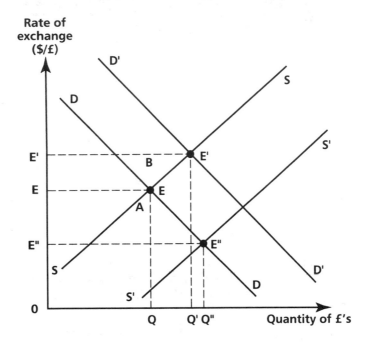

Figure 4.1

4 Changes in demand

In Figure 4.1 the shift in the demand for sterling from DD to D'D' has caused an increase in the equilibrium exchange rate relative to dollars from E to E'. Such a shift could be caused by:

- An increased preference amongst US citizens for British goods.
- An increase in incomes in the United States.
- Capital inflows to the UK.
- Speculation.

5 Changes in supply

An increase in imports into the UK from the USA would increase the supply of pounds, shown in Figure 4.1 as the shift in the supply curve from SS to S'S', with a consequent reduction in the equilibrium exchange rate from E to E".

6 Changes in the value of the pound

A fall in the value of the pound will, ceteris paribus:

- Raise the price of imports.
- Reduce the price of exports.

An increase in the value of the pound will, ceteris paribus:

- Reduce the price of imports.
- Raise the price of exports.

7 Purchasing power parity theory

This explains the equilibrium exchange rate between two currencies in terms of the price levels in the two countries. It states that the value of one currency relative to another depends upon the relative purchasing power of the two currencies in their domestic economies, i.e. the exchange rate will be determined at the point where the purchasing power of a unit of the currency is the same in each country. The theory can be expressed as follows:

$$\text{The price of the pound in dollars} = \frac{\text{US price level}}{\text{UK price level}}$$

This has important implications for the relationship between exchange rates and inflation. Although short-run deviations from purchasing power parity are possible, in the long run the theory probably does hold true.

8 Floating exchange rates

Floating, free or flexible exchange rates refer to an exchange rate system such as that described above where the equilibrium rate of exchange is determined by the forces of demand and supply on the foreign exchange market. The following characteristics of floating exchange rates should be borne in mind:

- A businessperson who enters a contract with an overseas supplier for delivery of goods at a future date with payment in foreign currency upon delivery never knows exactly how much they will have to pay as the exchange rate may be subject to fluctuation in the intervening period. Some argue that this tends to act as a deterrent to international trade. It is possible however to safeguard against currency fluctuations by buying currency ahead on the forward exchange market.
- In a free exchange rate system the action of speculators will tend to stabilise the currency around a long term trend as they buy the currency when it is weak and sell it when it is dear.
- Under a flexible exchange rate system the balance of payments should be self correcting. A deficit results in a fall in the exchange rate which reduces the price of UK exports and therefore demand increases. At the same time the increase in the price of imports should reduce some of the demand for imports. Eventually a balance of payments equilibrium should be re-established.

9 Fixed exchange rate

Fixed exchange rate systems are intended to remove the uncertainty associated with flexible rates. The fixed exchange rate system was introduced at the Bretton Woods conference in 1944 and was effective from 1947. The system was intended to bring stability to world trade and to stimulate its growth. The **International Monetary Fund** (IMF) was also established in order to assist countries with balance of payments difficulties. The fixed exchange rate system was finally abandoned in 1973.

Each currency was given a **par value** in terms of the dollar, e.g. £1 = $2.80 and the central bank of each country (in the UK the Bank of England) agreed to intervene on the foreign exchange markets in order to maintain the value of its currency 1 % either side of the par value, widened to 2¼% either side of par in 1971. In Figure 4.2 the par value is £1 = $2.40. As a result of an increase in imports the supply of pounds shifts from SS to S'S'and equilibrium shifts to E' with a new exchange rate at $2.00. However the central bank intervenes and buys pounds with gold or foreign currency shifting the demand from DD to D'D' with a new equilibrium at E" and the exchange rate returns to par value at $2.40. Had the exchange, rate risen to £1 = $3.00 the Bank of England would have intervened and sold pounds in order to increase the supply and return to the par value. An essential component of such a scheme is large reserves of gold and foreign currency. Under the scheme member countries could draw reserves from the IMF for this purpose when their currencies came under pressure.

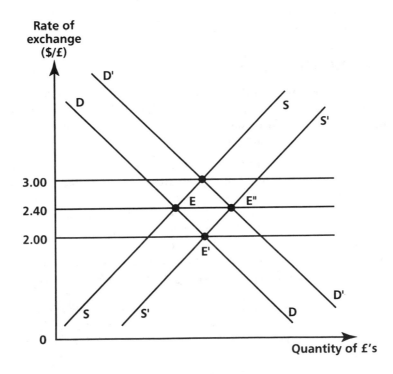

Figure 4.2

10 The advantages and disadvantages of a fixed system

The major **advantage** claimed for fixed exchange rates is that they eliminate uncertainty from international trade.

The alleged **disadvantages** of fixed exchange rates are:

- If the original rate is set too high, i.e. above the equilibrium rate, then it will be difficult to achieve a balance of payments equilibrium.
- Domestic policies for managing the economy are dominated by the need to maintain the external value of the currency.
- Fixed exchange rates are subject to extreme speculative pressures. The speculator has 'everything to gain and little to lose'. If he anticipates a **devaluation** of the sterling exchange rate and sells pounds, this can only add to the pressure for devaluation; after devaluation he can buy the pounds back at a lower rate. Even if the devaluation does not occur he is no worse off. In the event of an anticipated revaluation the purchase of pounds can only add to the pressure for revaluation, again if it does not come about the speculator has little to lose. The pound came under extreme pressure from speculators in the 1960s and early 1970s when the overvalued pound resulted in a series of balance of payments deficits.

11 Devaluation

Devaluation refers to the deliberate reduction of the exchange rate relative to other currencies in a fixed exchange rate system, the objective being to make exports more competitive terms of foreign currency whilst imports become more expensive. Under the fixed exchange rate system this was allowed where a nation was subject to recurring balance of payments difficulties. The UK devalued sterling in 1949 and in 1967. **Revaluation** refers to the decision to raise the par value of the exchange rate. Devaluation will not necessarily result in an improvement in the balance of payments however.

- If the demand for exports is **inelastic** then the devaluation may not raise total export earnings, and the desired improvement in the balance of payments will be even more difficult to achieve if the demand for imports is also **inelastic**.
- If other trading nations retaliate with a successive round of devaluations then the advantage gained from the devaluation will soon be lost.
- There must be sufficient excess capacity in the domestic economy to meet the increased demand for exports.

12 J-curve effect

The initial impact of a currency depreciation or devaluation may well be to cause a deterioration in the current account. In a manufacturing economy such as the UK this occurs because raw materials have to be imported at a higher cost than previously and in larger quantities if more goods are to be manufactured for export. Eventually the effect of the depreciation results in a higher level of exports, and domestic goods are substituted for imports, the current account then moves into surplus. This effect, known as the **J-curve effect**, is illustrated in Figure 4.3.

The depreciation at M initially results in a deterioration of the current account. At point N the effect of the depreciation begins to feed through to exports and the current account starts to improve, moving back into surplus at Q.

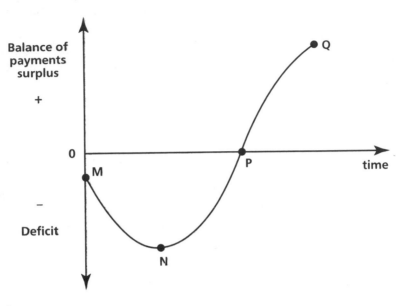

Figure 4.3

13 Depreciation and appreciation

Under a fixed exchange rate system devaluation tends to become confused with issues such as national pride, under a floating rate the exchange rate adjusts automatically to equilibrium with the domestic economy being less sensitive to changes in external demand. Under floating exchange rates a fall in the exchange rate is referred to as a **depreciation** and an increase in the exchange rate as an **appreciation**.

14 Effective exchange rate

The discussion of exchange rates so far has been in terms of the rate between the pound and the dollar, in reality of course the pound will be appreciating in terms of some currencies whilst depreciating against others, for example it may weaken against the yen and at the same time strengthen against the franc. In order to evaluate the overall change in the value of sterling a measure known as the effective exchange rate is used. The **effective exchange rate** (EER) shows the movements in sterling relative to a weighted average of the currencies of the UK's major trading partners. The movements in sterling are therefore measured against a 'basket' of other currencies and the importance (weight) of these currencies in the basket is determined by the amount of trade we conduct with that nation, i.e. it is 'trade weighted.' Recent movements in the sterling exchange rate and the EER are shown in Figures 4.4 and 4.5.

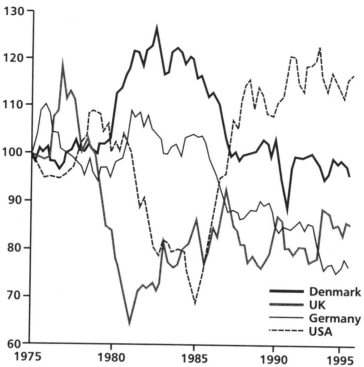

Figure 4.4
Real effective exchange rate, four countries 1975–95 (%, 1975 = 100%)

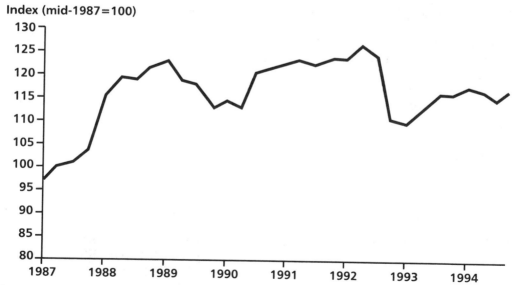

Figure 4.5
UK real effective exchange rate 1987–95

15 The end of the fixed exchange rate system

The devaluation of sterling in 1967 was the first crack in the fixed exchange rate system. Following this other currencies came under successive bouts of speculative pressure, and later with the onset of world recession, inflation, and the oil price crisis of 1973/74, the system became increasingly unstable. Despite various attempts to restore it, in particular the Smithsonian Institute agreement in 1971 and the attempt to establish a European Monetary System, sterling was allowed to float in June 1972 effectively signalling the end of the Bretton Woods system.

16 The EMS

The original proposals for a European Monetary System (EMS) were contained in the Werner Report of 1969 which advocated establishment of full European Monetary Union (EMU) by 1980. The establishment of the EMS was envisaged as a preliminary stage in the movement towards complete monetary union. The EMS came into operation on 13 March 1979, however, little further progress was made on the issue of monetary union until the publication of the report of the Delors Committee in April 1989. One of the proposals of the Delors Committee was that all European Community currencies should be within the EMS by 1 July 1990.

A key feature of the EMS is the European Currency Unit (ECU), which is intended to facilitate the operation of the Exchange Rate Mechanism (ERM). The ECU is a basket of EC currencies which act as a benchmark or 'numeraire' for the operation of the exchange-rate mechanism. The basket is a weighted average of the consituent currencies, with greater weights being given to more important currencies such as the deutschmark, and lower weights to the less important ones such as the Irish punt, Greek drachma and Luxembourg franc.

17 The ERM

The Exchange rate Mechanism (ERM) is a fixed exchange rate system within which each member currency is given a central rate against other EC currencies. Each currency is allowed to fluctuate by 2.5% either side of its central rate. When a currency reaches the intervention point of 2.25% above or below its par value the central banks intervene to maintain the value of the currency by buying it. The finance for this operation is available from the European Monetary Co-operation Fund. Intervention does not, however, take place without consultation between the EMS members who jointly determine intervention policy. Where a currency needs to be re-aligned it can be revalued or devalued by a joint policy decision of the members.

18 The disadvantages of the ERM

Prior to October 1990 the UK had participated in the establishment of the EMS and had participated in the EMCF and the ECU arrangements but had not joined the ERM. The reasons for the apparent reluctance of the UK government to join can be summarised as follows:

- The possibility of conflict between the Medium Term Financial Strategy (MTFS) which emphasises control of the money supply as its policy objective and the EMS which emphasises the exchange rate. Hence the government feared some loss of control over the money supply. Fixed exchange rate systems inevitably mean that internal economic policy becomes dominated by the need to maintain the external value of the currency, and hence there is some loss of control over domestic policy decisions.

- Experience of the Bretton Woods system resulted in fears that setting the exchange rates of economies with widely differencing economic performance within narrow limits would be ill-advised resulting in downward pressures on the currencies of the weaker economies.
- As an oil exporter, unlike the other member countries, the UK's interests may diverge widely from the interests of the other members and put intolerable strains on the ERM.

19 The advantages of the ERM

The purported advantages for the UK of membership of the ERM were those of fixed exchange rate systems in general; however, the main points in favour can be summarised as follows:

- It would form a 'zone of exchange rate stability' which would encourage trade between member countries.
- The UK would be forced to adopt policies which would keep inflation down to the level of that in Germany if the exchange rate is to be kept within the agreed band.
- Sterling would be subject to less speculative pressure, as with a more stable currency there would be less opportunity for speculative activities.
- With the greater stability in the sterling exchange rate it should be possible to reduce UK interest rates closer to those of the EU average.

20 Britain's membership of the ERM

Britain joined the ERM with effect from 7th October 1990 at the parity of £1 = DM 2.95 with the value to be maintained within a 6% band on either side of the par value. The value of the pound was to be maintained by the Bank of England, in conjunction with the other central banks of the EMS members, buying and selling pounds. If intervention on the money markets failed then interest rate policy was to be used as the next stage, and as a last resort application could be made for a realignment.

Fixed exchange rate systems inevitably mean that internal economic policy becomes dominated by the need to maintain the external value of the currency, and hence there is some loss of control over domestic policy decisions. The government's medium term financial strategy emphasised control of the money supply as its policy objective and the EMS emphasised the exchange rate.

This conflict over policy objectives impaled the government upon the horns of a major dilemma. As the UK economy slid into recession in 1991 pressure mounted for reductions in interest rates; this, together with a loss of confidence in the UK economy, resulted in the selling of sterling which drifted toward the bottom of its permitted range. By August 1992 the pound appeared hopelessly over-valued against the D-mark, the balance of payments was heavily into deficit and the domestic recession was deepening. In such a situation it would normally be expected to have a depreciating currency and reductions in interest rates. The commitment to the ERM however ruled out these options, and the risk of even higher interest rates mounted. On 16th September 1992 ('Black Wednesday') there was massive selling of sterling resulting in large scale intervention by the Bank of England to the tune of £13 billion of foreign currency and an increase in interest rates to 15%, without a recovery, resulting in the suspension of Britain's membership of the ERM the same day.

21 'Black Wednesday' and beyond

1993 saw further volatility, the Spanish peseta and the Portugese escudo were devalued further. The Danish krone experienced speculation as did the Belgian franc. This nearly destroyed the ERM. The result was that the ERM finance ministers declared 15% bands of fluctuation instead of the 2.25% bands. Although the ERM survived in principle the bands were so wide that they were thought to be rather meaningless.

Britain's view was to wait and see. However many believe, that rather than the 16th September 1992 being 'Black Wednesday' it did in fact produce beneficial effects for the UK. The large devaluation produced an export-led recovery and at the same time the government was allowed to use its monetary policy with greater effect, freed from the constraints of membership of the ERM.

22 EMU – The future

The crises of 1992 and 1993 seemed to signal the end of the EMU but in 1994 it returned to the political agenda. European Union leaders are preparing for a single currency, already named as the 'Euro', and predictions are that it will start in 1999. There has been debate and argument over the conditions for entry and France and Germany's commitment has been questioned.

Britain has negotiated an 'opt-out' agreement which requires the agreement of a future British government, with a majority. In return Britain has agreed not to prevent or influence other EU members joining a single European currency.

Self assessment questions

1 Distinguish between fixed and floating exchange rates.
2 Why was the fixed exchange rate system introduced?
3 What are the major disadvantages of fixed exchange rates?
4 Distinguish between a devaluation and a depreciation of a currency.
5 In what circumstances would devaluation result in an improvement in the balance of payments?
6 In the absence of official intervention in the foreign exchange market, what factors are likely to influence changes in a country's exchange rate?
7 Examine the courses of action open to a country faced with a deficit on its balance of payments.
8 On a given day the demand for, and supply of, sterling in the foreign exchange market are as follows:–

Exchange rates

Price of sterling (in francs)	11.50	11.80	12.10	13.00
Sterling demanded (£ million)	25	22	20	17
Sterling supplied (£ million)	15	17	20	22

(a) What will be the equilibrium exchange rate?

(b) Britain's trade figures show a deficit, and demand for sterling falls by £5 million. What is the new equilibrium exchange rate?

(c) In these new circumstances the British authorities decide to peg the exchange rate at £1 = 12.10 francs. What steps must they take?

(d) If the exchange rate was successfully pegged at £1 = 12.10 francs, would sterling be over-valued or undervalued?

5

Unemployment

1 Labour

Labour is the least durable of all resources; a day's output lost due to unemployment is lost permanently and cannot be regained. Unemployment therefore has high economic costs, but in addition the costs in terms of misery and despair cannot be ignored.

2 Types of unemployment

In order to formulate appropriate policies to cure unemployment it is necessary to identify precisely the type of unemployment which is being dealt with as the policy instruments appropriate to the cure of one type may not be appropriate to another. It is usual to classify the employment as one of four types: **seasonal**; **frictional**; **structural** and **cyclical (deficient demand)**.

3 Seasonal unemployment

Some industries are highly seasonal in character and the levels of unemployment in such industries therefore also tends to fluctuate with the seasons, e.g. the hotel and catering industry in resorts, fruit picking, and the construction industry, are all affected particularly by climatic changes.

4 Frictional unemployment

This results from the frictions in the labour market which occur due to labour immobility, or the process of searching for job information. Even at what is normally deemed to be full employment there would still be an element of frictional unemployment because it takes time and resources for workers to change jobs. There may be an adequate number of vacancies but it takes time for a suitable match between those seeking employment and appropriate vacancies to be found.

5 Structural unemployment

This type of unemployment arises out of more fundamental changes in the industrial base of the economy. It is associated with the decline of 'staple' industries and the problem arises because as industries decline the skills required for them become obsolete also. This becomes a serious problem because these industries tend to be concentrated in certain **regions** and when these industries decline **regional decline** occurs as a consequence. Examples include: shipbuilding in the North West, North East, Glasgow and northern Ireland; cotton textiles in the North West; iron and steel making in south Wales and the north east, and some of the coal fields in the North West, the Midlands and the North. Vacancies may exist in the economy but they may be in different areas and involve different skills. The concentration of unemployment in the regions becomes a problem due to:

- The occupational immobility of labour – the unwillingness to abandon skills and acquire new ones.
- The geographical immobility of labour – workers are reluctant to move to vacancies elsewhere due to cultural, family and financial ties to the regions. Structural decline may result from some or all of the following:
  - Technological change.
  - The development of substitutes, e.g. the effect of man-made fibres such as nylon on the cotton industry.
  - The growth of overseas competition.

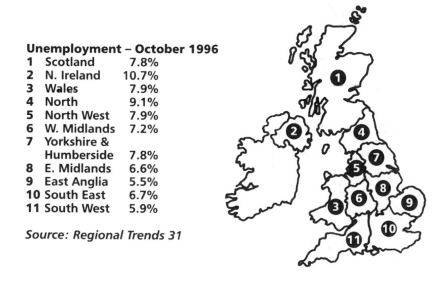

Unemployment – October 1996

1	Scotland	7.8%
2	N. Ireland	10.7%
3	Wales	7.9%
4	North	9.1%
5	North West	7.9%
6	W. Midlands	7.2%
7	Yorkshire & Humberside	7.8%
8	E. Midlands	6.6%
9	East Anglia	5.5%
10	South East	6.7%
11	South West	5.9%

Source: Regional Trends 31

Figure 5.1

6 Regional unemployment

Figure 5.1 illustrates the regional variation in unemployment rates. The reluctance of labour to move from the regions has resulted in the alternative policy of moving 'work to the workers' in the form of **regional policy**, under which governments have used a variety of measures in order to encourage firms to expand into the regions of high unemployment. (See Chapter 6).

7 Cyclical unemployment

This type of unemployment results from a general deficiency of total demand in the economy (This is dealt with in more detail in Chapter 12).

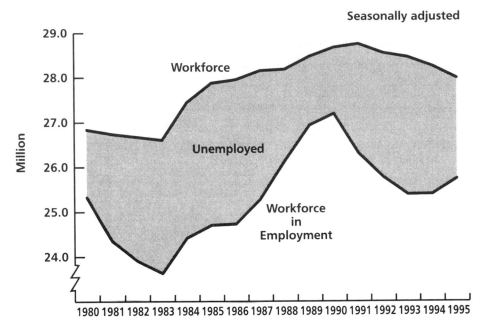

Figure 5.2

8 Unemployment trends

There were in 1992 almost as many unemployed as there were in 1984, and three times as many as in the 1950s. Three further important points to note regarding recent unemployment.

- The increase in unemployment among the young.
- An increase in the duration of unemployment.
- The period of rising unemployment has coincided with an increase in the size of the working population, as can be seen in Figure 30.2.
- A continued reduction in the numbers employed in manufacturing industry (see Figure 30.4) and an increase in those employed in non-manufacturing.

In January 1993 unemployment peaked at 3 million (seasonally adjusted) in the UK, this represented 10.6% of the workforce. A large proportion of these had been unemployed for more than a year. The highest level of unemployment prior to this had been in 1984 with approximately 13% of the workforce unemployed.

Since January 1993 the jobless total has fallen consistently and by the end of 1996 the official figure was 2 million or 7.2% of the workforce. All of the regions of the country have enjoyed a fall in unemployment with the largest being experienced in the South West, the West Midlands and the South East.

This fall in the level of unemployment has been attributed to the economic recovery that has taken place in the UK. It should however be born in mind that the official government statistics are unreliable, as the methods used for counting unemployment have been changed 31 times since 1979. Most of these changes have reduced the published unemployed total by a significant amount. This makes any comparison over time very difficult.

The result of this has been that the UK government now produces two different series of unemployment data, the claim count (the figures produced above) and the labour survey.

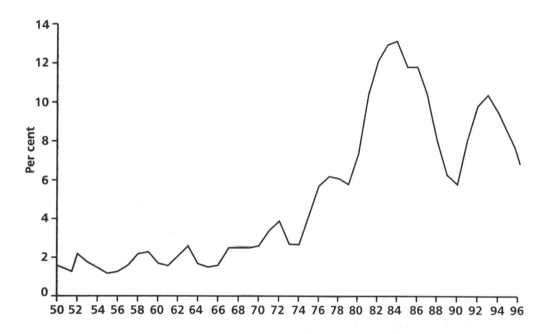

Figure 5.3 UK unemployment 1950–96

Self assessment questions

1 How does frictional unemployment occur and why is it a less serious problem than other forms of unemployment?

2 Why does structural unemployment create a problem for the regions?

3 What is meant by regional policy and why have governments in the past felt that they needed such a policy?

4 In what sense is unemployment a waste of resources?

5 As an economy develops what changes would you expect to take place within its occupational structure?

6 State the main categories of unemployment and indicate those which are the main concern of government economic policy.

6
Regional policy

1 Regional imbalances

The regional imbalance of incomes and employment which arises from the decline of the staple industries in the regions has resulted in the devising of various measures aimed at reducing these regional disparities. These measures, generally referred to as **regional policy**, attempt to encourage the growth of industry in the regions. Government intervention in this context arises from the desire for the greater economic growth which will result from a fuller utilisation of resources, both labour and capital; and a desire for greater equality of employment and incomes. Because of the reluctance of labour to move to areas of high employment measures generally attempt to influence the firm's location decision, i.e. 'bring work to the workers', by a combination of measures aimed at reducing the firm's costs if they locate in specified areas or by prohibiting through planning regulations expansion elsewhere (the 'carrot and stick' approach).

2 The regional map

The present pattern of assistance was established in the 1972 Industry Act, although regional policy originated in the 1930s and expanded rapidly in the 1960s. The extent of assistance available varies according to the designation of the area. Prior to November 1984 there were three categories of development area:

- **Special development areas (SDAs).**
- **Development areas (DAs).**
- **Intermediate areas (IAs).**

SDAs were the areas with the most serious problems of structural decline such as Merseyside, Clydeside and Newcastle, and these received the greatest assistance. The scale of assistance was less in the DAs and IAs. Northern Ireland was categorised as a **Special Development Area**, receiving additional assistance because of the unique problems of that region. In November 1984 the category of special development area was dispensed with and the map was redrawn. In 1993 a new 'map' of assisted areas was produced by the government. Once again it used a ranking of areas in terms of aid priority.

This had only two categories for assistance as with the 1984 map:

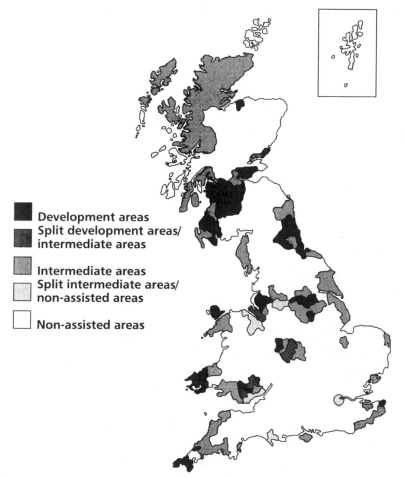

Figure 6.1

- Development areas.
- Intermediate areas.

Some areas were also designated as 'split' areas, these fell between the criteria used for DAs and IAs.

Another significant change was the inclusion of areas in the south east such as London (Park Royal and the Lea Valley), Clacton, Dover, Folkstone and the Isle of Wight.

The distribution of the development areas is illustrated in Figure 6.1.

3 Instruments of regional policy

The main instruments of regional policy are as follows:

Prior to March 1988 the main instrument of regional policy was the regional development grant (RDG). The RDG was a capital grant of 15% payable to firms in the development areas on investment in plant, buildings and machinery. The grants were subject to a cost per job limit of £10,000. Alternatively a job grant was made available of £3,000 for each new job created in labour intensive projects. In the 1988 White Paper, the

DTI stated that automatic eligibility for the RDG was to cease, in the 1990s it has been greatly reduced.

Capital grants were subject to the criticism that they encouraged capital intensive production when the underlying purpose was the creation of jobs. Also the grants failed to discriminate between good and bad investment; moreover the grant would be paid to firms who would have made the investment even if the grant did not exist.

To overcome some of these criticisms the government introduced in March 1988 **The Regional Initiative** with a new system of **regional enterprise grants.** These grants are given at the discretion of the Department of Trade and Industry (DTI) upon the presentation of a **business plan** by the applicant and are no longer automatically available. The grants will be provided only if the business plan meets the criteria of the DTI and the project is taking place in a Development Area or South Yorkshire.

The criteria applied include: market opportunities for the business over the next 2–3 years, the effect of the project on sales, profits and employment levels, and how the project and the business will be financed.

The grants are of two types:

- Grants for **investment** projects in most manufacturing and some service sectors. The DTI will pay 15% of expenditure on fixed assets in the project, up to a maximum grant of £15,000. Eligible costs include plant and machinery (new or second-hand), buildings, purchase of land and site preparation, and vehicles used solely on site.
- Grants for **innovation** projects which lead to the development and introduction of new or improved products and processes. The DTI will pay 50% of eligible costs, up to a maximum grant of £25,000. Work can range from feasibility studies, through the development of technical specifications, to the design and manufacture of prototypes. There is no limit on the size of projects which can be considered.

The measures introduced in March 1988, and built upon in 1993, represented a significant movement towards a more market orientated approach to regional policy.

- The provision of '**advance factories**' for sale or rent on favourable terms. These were standard factory units constructed by a division of the Department of Trade and Industry which were immediately available for firms to move into. However recently the emphasis has been on smaller units ('Busybee Workshops') in order to encourage the growth of new businesses.
- **Enterprise zones.** These represent an attempt to deal with the problems of the inner cities and go beyond what is strictly regional policy as some of them lie outside the development areas. The concept reflects the view held by the previous government that excessive controls and regulations can stifle initiative. The zones are specified areas mainly within the larger cities where special provisions apply in order to encourage industrial and commercial activity. At present there are 25 such zones in areas such as Merseyside (Speke), Midlands (Corby & Dudley), Northern Ireland (Belfast), Greater Manchester (Salford Docks and Trafford Park), Tyneside (Newcastle and Gateshead), London (Isle of Dogs). The main incentives in the enterprise zones are as follows:
  - Exemption from development land tax for 10 years.
  - 100% capital allowances (for corporation and income tax purposes) for commercial and industrial buildings.
  - Exemption from rates on industrial and commercial property for 10 years.

- Simplified and relaxed regulations for planning procedures.
- Simpler and speedier administration of remaining controls, and government requests for statistical information is to be kept to a minimum.
- **Regional selective assistance.** This is a variety of further grants available for capital and training costs where it can be shown that jobs will be created.
- **Industrial development certificates (IDCs).** These represented a form of administrative control on industrial development outside the assisted areas. An IDC was required for all new factories or extensions, and by refusing to grant an IDC for anywhere outside a development area pressure could be exerted to ensure that development took place within the development areas. The use of IDC's as a policy instrument was abolished as it was seen as interference by the government in the market mechanism, (see 5).

4 The European Union (EU)

In the 1990s the EU has become a significant part of the UK's regional policy. The European Regional Development Fund makes loans to central and local government for spending on capital and infrastructure projects. The European Social Fund also provides funds for the regeneration of areas with particular social problems which usually originate from high levels of unemployment.

This has provided new capital for the regions in the UK and a whole range of new initiatives. Three areas of the UK – Northern Ireland, the Highlands and Islands and Merseyside qualified for £2 billion of expenditure from the EU's structural funds over the period 1994–97. This money is not given to individual firms but made available to the government.

5 The free market approach

The **free market approach** to the regional problem suggests that any interference in the location decisions of firms will lead to location decisions which are non optimal and therefore inefficient. The firm makes its location decision on the basis of cost minimisation and any interference with this process, it is suggested will result in a location being chosen which is not the best one in terms of economic efficiency.

Advocates of the free-market approach suggest that the **regional problem will solve itself if left to market forces**. Regional unemployment merely indicates a labour market disequilibrium with an excess supply of labour at the prevailing wage rates and all that is required is a reduction in wages which will then be reflected in lower product prices and equilibrium will be re-established in the labour market. Labour and capital should be free to make their own decisions regarding location and if unemployment is high in a region then wage rates will be lower and some labour will be attracted to other more prosperous regions by the higher wage rates. Also at some point in time the lower wage rates in the declining regions will begin to attract firms who realise that by locating there they can reduce their wage costs and ultimately increase their profits. Eventually this movement of labour and capital will re-establish an equilibrium situation with full employment. If labour is unwilling to move then there must be some other advantages which equalise the employment disadvantages; the same is also true of firms who are unwilling to move voluntarily into the regions.

The market approach is generally advocated by those who believe that government intervention in the market should be minimal if economic efficiency is to be achieved.

Advocates of the free market approach also suggest that there are further burdens imposed by government intervention in the form of taxation, subsidisation, and the imposition of bureaucratic controls.

6 The arguments against the free market approach

Opponents of the market approach however point to a number of weaknesses in that principle:

- **The time scale involved** in the re-establishment of a new equilibrium situation may be very lengthy as the comparative advantage in production between regions is likely to change only slowly.
- **Social costs** may be imposed in both the areas of expansion and of contraction. In the declining regions as labour departs there will be costs imposed by the underutilisation of existing facilities such as schools and hospitals which will fall into decline as the regional income falls. In the expanding areas there will be a shortage of such social facilities with a high level of demand for those facilities which do exist. There are also likely to be the problems of inner-city decay and falling property prices in the declining regions, with shortages of accommodation and rapidly rising prices in the areas of growth. There may also be additional costs from congestion as roads and transport facilities are used more intensively in the growth areas. The disparity in house prices between the North of England and the South-East are a case in point.
- The market solution ignores the **hardship and suffering imposed** upon those involved, which may be so extreme that governments may find it politically unacceptable.
- As labour leaves the declining region the population falls, reducing the size of the potential market for new firms in the region. The departure of labour and firms also reduces local expenditure, and therefore incomes, resulting in further unemployment in the ancillary industries such as retailing and distribution. This further decline in incomes is referred to as the regional multiplier and makes it less likely that firms will locate in the declining regions. The opposite is the case in the expanding regions where the **regional multiplier** sets in train a circle of rising incomes and prosperity and is likely to be a factor in attracting firms to the more prosperous regions.
- The assumption that the labour market operates in a frictionless manner must also be questioned in the light of **nationwide collective bargaining.** Nationwide collective bargaining has the effect of reducing regional wage differences. Where national representatives of a trade union negotiate a national wage rate for their membership then the sensitivity of wage rates to regional differences in employment will be reduced.

7 Regional policy effectiveness

The effectiveness of regional policy is difficult to quantify, however, many studies indicate that regional unemployment is worse in the absence of policy

An official paper, 'The Movement of Manufacturing Industry in the UK, 1945–65' which was updated in 1981 showed that during the period 1945–81 the South East lost 1,647 manufacturers and the West Midlands 334. During the same period 586 manufacturers were gained in Wales, 365 in the North, 354 in East Anglia and 316 in the South

West. This clearly shows the success of regional policy.

A 1986 DTI paper estimated that 784,000 jobs were created in the assisted areas between 1960 and 1981. By the end of 1981, even after a hard recession 600,000 jobs remained. This of course ignores the cost of these jobs and the social costs and benefits involved.

In contrast the market based approach of the 1990s showed the regional unemployment differentials widening and a decrease in the participation rates of the depressed areas.

Regional differences in employment and income are still substantial despite assistance. The South East also appears to have a greater comparative advantage in the modern growth industries, especially since the opening of the channel tunnel.

8 Inner city programmes

The problem of the inner cities has been the focus of the greatest attention since the late 1980s. Inner city areas, particularly in the North of England, frequently have very high levels of unemployment, inferior housing, poverty, declining public servlces and a poor environment generally. The reasons for this deterioration are complex but the decline of manufacturing industry has been a major factor, also the age of the housing stock and the development of new business areas in more pleasant areas with better access to motorways. Many initiatives have been used by the government to assist the inner cities and some of the main schemes are listed below. A point which should be noted is that several of the schemes rely on partnerships between central and local government and private industry.

- **The Urban Programme,** implemented by the Department of the Environment, allocates money to local authorities and community groups. The money is spent on training schemes for the unemployed, factory renovation, small factory units and provision of community centres.
- **Enterprise zones** (discussed above under regional policy) are directed primarily at the inner city areas.
- **Task forces**, established by the Department of Employment provide special help to the most badly deprived areas, some of which have suffered rioting and public disorder. The task forces consist of small teams of civil servants based in deprived areas who draw aid from existing programmes and from the private sector and local authorities and concentrate the assistance into these areas.
- **Urban Development Corporations (UDCs)** have been playing an increasingly important role in the inner cities. They have extensive powers and can buy and sell land, build factories and offices; they can renovate sub-standard property, convert property to alternative uses, e.g. warehouses into flats or offices. One of their main objectives is the attraction of private capital back into the inner cities with the idea of making the environment more attractive generally in the hope that new industries will develop in addition to housing. The dockland developments in London and Liverpool are notable examples of the work of two UDCs.
- A number of local authorities established local employment initiatives, for example economic development units to co-ordinate policy initiatives to gain the maximum effect, and enterprise boards which invest directly in property and business.

9 The future

In reality the choice lies not between the two extreme views of the free market and the planned location approach, but in the selection of the most appropriate mix. In recent years less emphasis has been placed on regional policy with a move towards a more market-orientated solution despite the increasing contribution of the EU. There is however still an important role for the policy for the regions.

Self assessment questions

1 Why is there a 'regional problem'?

2 What are the main instruments of UK regional policy?

3 Outline the market approach to the regional problem.

4 What are the main problems involved with the market approach to the regional problem?

5 Discuss the problems created by the tendency of labour to be immobile. What measures can government adopt in order to resolve these problems?

7

Taxation

1 Origins of taxation

Taxes were originally-levied for the purposes of raising **revenue**, in a modern economy; however, they are also used as a means of regulating the level of total (aggregate) demand (see Chapter 12), redistributing incomes and wealth, and regulating markets.

2 'Canons' of taxation

Adam Smith stated that the four 'canons' (principles) of taxation were as follows:

- **Equity**
- **Certainty**
- **Efficiency**
- **Convenience**

Equity refers to the principle that taxes should generally be seen to be fair.
Certainty refers to the principles that the taxpayers should know their tax liability in advance and that the government should know their revenue in advance.
Efficiency refers to the principle that a good tax will be economic to administer and the costs of administration should be a small proportion of the tax revenue.
Convenience refers to the principle that taxes should be levied at a time and place convenient to the taxpayer.

3 Additional criteria

In a modern economy there are a number of additional criteria for an efficient tax system.

- **Neutrality** – Taxes should as far as possible be neutral, i.e. not distort the price mechanism. The way in which resources were allocated prior to the introduction of the tax should be the same afterwards. Direct taxation is generally held to be superior in terms of neutrality than indirect taxation. The cost to the economy in terms of resource misallocation, which is incurred as a consequence of indirect taxation, is referred to as the excess burden of indirect taxation. The excess burden is greatest the more indirect taxes change the relative prices of goods.

- **Stabilisation** – Taxes should be efficient from the point of view of their use in regulating the level of aggregate demand in the economy (see Chapter 12). It is useful if a small tax change has a significant effect on demand, this however may conflict with the neutrality principle.
- **Incentive/disincentive effect** – The extent to which the tax is an incentive or disincentive to work, save, and invest.
- **Flexibility** and **stability** – The speed with which tax laws can be changed, and those changes implemented.
- **Redistribution of income and wealth** – The effectiveness of the tax system in creating a more equal distribution of income and wealth.

4 PAYE

Pay As You Earn (PAYE) income tax is an example of a tax which conforms closely to each of the four principles. The tax rates are **progressive** so the higher paid pay a higher tax rate than the lower paid. Tax rates are published and the tax rate made known to the taxpayer. The tax is efficient as the collection of the tax is the responsibility of the employer, who deducts it from incomes and pays it to the Inland Revenue. It is convenient for the taxpayer as it is deducted at source by the employer.

5 Direct taxes

These are borne by those responsible for paying the tax and are levied on either incomes or wealth and are collected by the Inland Revenue. Direct taxes include:

- Income tax: levied on personal income.
- Corporation tax: levied on company profits.
- Inheritance tax: chargeable on gifts, including property, transferred upon death or within seven years of death.
- Capital gains tax: levied on the increase in the value of assets between their acquisition and sale.
- National insurance contributions; although not formally regarded as a direct tax are a direct deduction from income.

6 Indirect taxes

Taxes on goods. The incidence (burden) of the tax may be passed on through higher prices to the buyer of the goods. The distribution of the tax incidence is related to the relative elasticities of demand and supply.

In Figure 7.1(a) a per unit sales tax of a–b shifts the supply curve from S to S^1, the vertical distance being the equivalent of the tax. The price to the consumer increases to p^2, in this instance the incidence of the tax is borne equally by the producer and the consumer, i.e. the consumer pays $p^1 - p^2$ of the tax and the producer pays $p^3 - p^1$, because the elasticity of demand and supply are approximately unity. The tax revenue is represented by the rectangle p^3p^2ba and the producers revenue is the rectangle $OP^3 aQ^2$. The triangle abc is referred to as **'deadweight loss'** and is a loss to society as a whole. In Figure 7.1(b) demand is inelastic and as a result more of the tax burden is passed on to the consumer, here the consumer pays $p^1 - p^2$ of the tax and the producer absorbs only p^3p^1. (Students should also experiment with different supply elasticities). Indirect taxes include:

- Value added tax (VAT): a percentage tax on consumer expenditure.
- Excise duties: are duties levied on domestically produced goods. They are generally specific taxes in that they are charged in the form of a sum per unit, e.g. petrol duty is levied on each gallon Other goods subject to excise duties include cigarettes, beer and spirits. These goods are subject to additional taxation because they tend to be in inelastic demand so that the tax does not reduce consumption significantly and the yield of

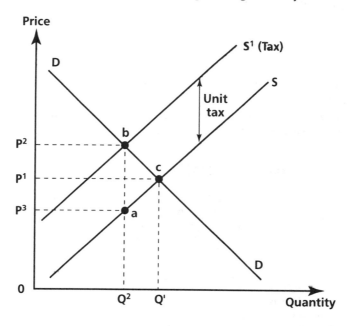

Figure 7.1(a)

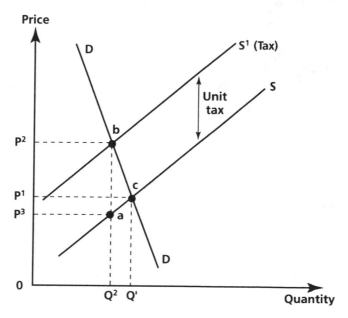

Figure 7.1(b)

the tax is maintained. Such goods may also bear additional tax because there may be an element of 'paternalism' in that governments may wish to curb excess consumption.
- Customs duties are taxes placed on imported goods. These may be imposed both for revenue purposes and for the protection of domestic industries. (See Chapter 2)
- Motor vehicles duties.
- Petroleum revenue tax (PRT) levied on the profits from obtaining oil and gas within the UK or its territorial sea. This has become an increasingly important source of revenue as a consequence of North Sea oil discoveries.

7 Regressive taxes

Regressive taxes are taxes which fall more heavily on the poor than the rich and therefore contravene the equity principle. Indirect taxes are generally held to be regressive. For example, if the duty on a bottle of whisky is £3, for a person earning £30 the tax rate is 10% of income but for a person earning £300 it is only 1% of income. A lump sum tax on income is the most regressive form of income tax. (See Figure 7.2)

8 Proportionate taxes

Proportionate taxes are a constant percentage of income, e.g. 10% of income. Corporation tax is an example of a proportionate tax in the UK as it is levied on companies as a percentage of profit. If it is accepted that the marginal utility of money declines then

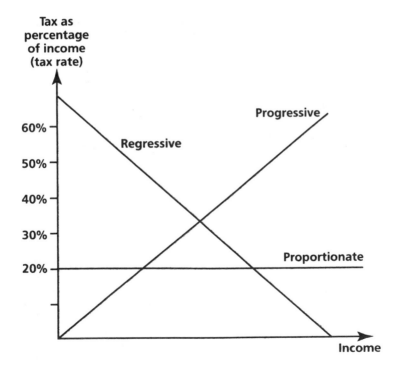

Figure 7.2

proportionate taxation of incomes is inequitable as the sacrifice of 10% of income by a person on a low income is a greater sacrifice than it is to somebody on a high income. (See Figure 7.2)

9 Progressive taxes

Progressive taxes are taxes where the tax rate increases as income rises and different 'slices' of income are taxed at different rates. As a consequence the proportion of income paid in tax becomes greater the higher the income. Progressive taxes therefore fall most heavily on higher incomes and are generally held to be the most equitable method of taxation. It has long been an accepted contention that taxation should be related to **ability to pay** on the grounds of **equity** (fairness) between individuals. This inevitably leads to consideration of the **tax rate** and two approaches can be identified.

- **Equality of sacrifice**: that the total burden on the nation should be equalized between individuals.
- **The benefit principle:** that people should be taxed according to the benefit they receive from the tax system.

Progressive taxation of incomes can be justified on the grounds of **equality of sacrifice**, given the assumption that the **marginal utility of money declines,** e.g. taking £1 in tax from a person earning £100 per week does not involve the same sacrifice of utility as taking £1 from a person earning £1000 per week. The major disadvantage which is claimed for the progressive taxation of incomes is that they operate as a **disincentive** to work and effort. (See 15)

10 The disincentive effect and the marginal rate of tax

The disincentive effect of progressive taxation will be greater the greater the marginal rate of taxation, i.e. the steeper the rate of progression. The disincentive effect can therefore be reduced by having wider tax bands and a lower rate of progression. The average rate of tax is defined as the total taxes paid divided by income, and the closer the average rate (or effective rate) of tax is to the marginal rate the lower will be the disincentive effect.

Figure 7.3 illustrates marginal and average rates of tax. The marginal rate of taxation is steep, hence an increase in income from Y to Y^l results in a substantial increase in tax paid on the additional income $(Y-Y^l)$ which may in theory act as a disincentive to work harder in order to increase income from Y to Y^l. The marginal and average tax rates are wide apart indicating the marked disincentive effect of this tax structure. Table 7.1 illustrates the income tax rates for 1976–77, 1985–86, 1988/89 and the rates introduced in the November 1996 budget. The simplified tax structure introduced in March 1988 was intended to create a simple two rate tax system which reduced the highest rates of tax, increased the starting point for everyone, and reduced the marginal rate for the majority of tax payers. In the 1997/98 tax structure the basic rate of income tax is 23% with a single higher tax rate of 40% for taxable incomes over £26,100 and a starting rate of 20% for the first £4,100 of taxable income. In Table 7.1 the move towards fewer, broader tax bands is clear as is the decrease in the basic rate of tax:

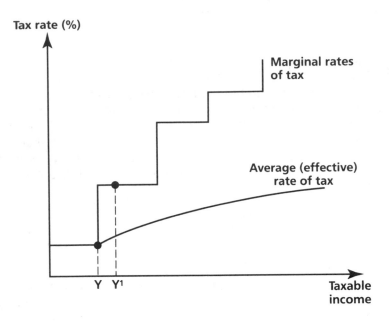

Tax rate (%)

Marginal rates
of tax

Average (effective)
rate of tax

Y Y¹

Taxable
income

Figure 7.3

An additional measure has been to gradually reduce the basic rate of tax and reduce the rate at which people begin to pay tax.

The changes in the structure are intended to remove the disincentive to work purported to be inherent in a progressive tax structure and to give greater incentives to those on higher incomes Care must be taken when comparing the four periods due to the effect of inflation on money incomes between the three periods.

In particular for those on low incomes consideration of the disincentive to work has to include consideration of the whole **tax system** including the receipt of benefits. For an unemployed worker the taking of a job may mean loss not only of unemployment benefit but benefits such as free school meals for children, rent subsidies etc.; the loss of these benefits can be considered as a form of **implicit tax.** The loss of benefits combined with positive income tax payments may act as a disincentive to the unemployed to take lower paid jobs, referred to as the **unemployment trap**. The ratio of unemployment benefit and/or supplementary benefit relative to post tax earnings is referred to as the **replacement ratio.** In theory a rise in the replacement ratio would result in an increase in unemployment and act as a disincentive to the unemployed to take low paid jobs; the evidence, however, is that the replacement ratio has in fact fallen over the last ten years and cannot therefore be a contributory factor to unemployment, although some commentators such as Professor Minford suggest that if the analysis is applied to the non unionised sector of the workforce only, then a substantial disincentive effect is evident. (See Chapter 17). Wider tax bands at the basic rate represent one measure aimed at overcoming this affect; others include reduced benefits or the use of negative income tax systems.

TABLE 7.1

Income	1976/77 Tax Rate %
0 – 5,000	35
5,001 – 5,500	40
5,501 – 6,500	45
6501 – 7,500	50
7,501 – 8,500	55
8,501 – 10,000	60
10,001 – 12,000	65
12,001 – 15,000	70
15,001 – 20,000	75
20,001 and over	83

Max 83% where total income after subtracting personal allowance and reliefs exceeds £20,000.

	1985/86
0 – 16,200	30
16,201 – 19,200	40
19,201 – 24,400	45
24,001 – 32,300	50
32,301 – 40,200	55
40,201 and over	6-

	1988/89
0 – 19,300	25
19,301 and over	40

	1997/98
0 – 4,100	20
4,101 – 26,100	23
26,101 and above	40

11 Negative income tax

Negative income tax systems guarantee a minimum income with benefits given as a right to all those below the minimum. As income increases towards a break-even point the size of benefit diminishes, and as the income recipients pass through the break-even point they become positive tax payers. In order to remove any disincentive effect the transition from being a recipient of benefit to a net taxpayer should be as smooth as possible. In Figure 7.4 the minimum income (or poverty line) is O–G, meaning that an individual earning no income would receive benefit payment O–G. As employment income rises benefit payments fall hence a person earning income M would receive benefit M–N (OL) thus total income is OMN. The break-even point is at E beyond which income recipients become positive tax payers. The positive tax rate EA is quite steep and may act as a disincentive to employment at the marginal income E or above. For example, if a person received a gross income of OY net income would be Y^1 (OY–XY). One suggested way of overcoming this is to have initially a lower positive marginal tax rate such as E–B, before moving to high marginal tax rates. In the example quoted this would leave a net income Y^2 if gross income was OY (Y^2 = OY - YZ). Various schemes have been suggested but they all claim the advantages of certainty, benefit being given as a right, ease of calculation, the concentrating of help where it is most needed, and the reduction of disincentives to take employment. The evidence regarding the disincentive affects of income tax is however inconclusive and it is possible that income taxes may in fact make some individuals actually work harder in order to maintain their post-tax incomes.

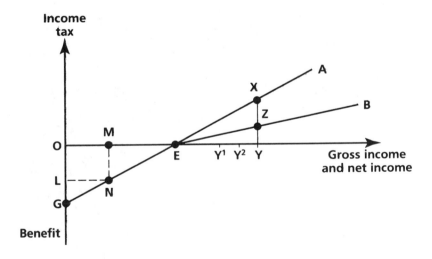

Figure 7.4

12 Corporation Tax

Corporation tax is a tax on company profits. Treating companies and shareholders as different entities enables the authorities to pursue different policies for the company and personal sectors of the economy. The **classical system** of corporation tax which was used in the UK up to 1973 taxed retained profits at a different rate to dispersed profits (dividends). One of the objectives of this policy was to use the tax system to influence the level of retained profits and therefore investment and consequently was not a neutral tax. Since April 1973 the **imputation system** has been used and under this system all profits whether distributed or not, are subject to the same corporation-tax rate, but part of the tax is 'imputed' to shareholders, and collected from the company at the time of payment of dividends. The 1984 budget reformed corporation tax by reducing the main rate from 52 per cent to 35 per cent by 1986, the reduction of the small companies rate to 30 per cent, and the phasing out over three years of stock relief, of first year capital allowances for plant and machinery and initial allowances for industrial building. For 1997/98 the main rate was 33% with the small company rate at 23%.The reason for making these changes was the belief that the old system of allowances subsidised and encouraged investment projects with low rates of return and that the new system would improve the business environment by taxing profits less and relaxing the amount of subsidation of investment.

13 Property tax

In the UK the traditional **property tax** has been the **rates**. The idea of rates is that they are a local tax used to provide local provision of goods and services by local authorities. Rates together with grants from central government were the main sources of revenue for local authorities. Rates were payable on the 'rateable value' of property which, was in principle equal to the yearly rent which could be obtained on the property. The actual amount payable, however, depended not only on the rateable value but also on the rate in the pound charged by the local authority which was calculated by dividing the sum to be raised to cover expenditures by the yield of a one pence rate to give the tax rate (or poundage).

Although rates were administratively easy to collect and difficult to avoid they were subject to the criticism that they were inequitable because they were not related to income and were therefore a regressive tax, i.e. they contravene the ability to pay principle. Also they were not paid by everyone within the household. A further criticism was that rates lacked buoyancy in that they did not rise automatically with income and the periodic substantial revaluations which this necessitated proved highly unpopular with rate payers. Business rates were criticised on the grounds that they were related to local authority expenditure plans rather that profitability.

The argument that rates were regressive may however not be as strong if wealth is taken as the basis and property size is taken as an indicator of wealth.

In response to the criticisms of rates the UK government replaced rates with a '**community charge**' which was a flat rate poll tax on every adult in the local authority jurisdiction. The community charge was introduced in March 1989 in Scotland and March 1990 in England and Wales. The principle underlying the charge was that it would make local authorities more responsive to the wishes of the local community in their expenditure and would be more like a charge for the services received than a lump sum tax. It proved to be the most short-lived and costly tax ever to be introduced. The tax proved to be highly unpopular due to its regressive nature resulting in massive non-payment. This coupled with the difficulties and costs of administration and the political unpopularity resulted in the abandonment of the 'poll tax' and its replacement from April 1993 with a new council tax. The cost of the community charge fiasco to the Treasury has been estimated at £7 billion per year.

14 Council tax

The council tax is based on property capital values, determined by approved estate agents/valuers, making use of a system of banding. The valuer determines which of eight bands of predetermined value a property falls in. A different rate of tax determined by the local authority is then applied to each band. The household rather than the individual will be the tax unit, with single person households receiving a 25% discount, and a rebate system maintained for those on low incomes.

- The council tax can be characterised as a combination of property tax, or old rating system, with a per capita element being retained. An element of progression is achieved through the valuation of property.
- The council tax, as a property tax, is strong administratively, but weak on efficiency and equity and unclear in terms of accountability.
- A problem exists due to the fact that in the south-east almost everyone will reside in property in one of the highest bands, whilst in the north there will be a far greater concentration in the lower bands. Consequently the tax provides little recognition of ability to pay within some areas and may be perceived by many as being another flat rate tax like the community charge.
- The provision of discounts to single householders requires authorities to carry out checks and set up a register, a costly exercise which is potentially as unpopular as that associated with the community charge.
- The valuation of property also has the potential for causing disruption. Householders have the right of appeal against valuations, and as many properties were valued before the fall in property values many appeals and protests were caused.

15 The Laffer curve

The discussion relating to taxation as a disincentive to effort is a supply-side concept that owes much to the worth of Arthur Laffer. His work produced the **Laffer curve** (see Figure 7.5) which argues that if taxes rates are zero then tax revenues will also be zero. Equally if tax rates are 100% the tax revenue will also be zero because individuals will refuse to work or will work illegally.

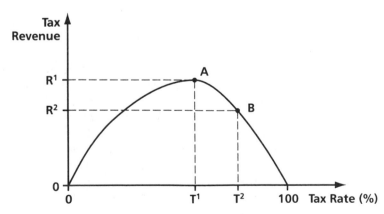

Figure 7.5

Between these rates lies an ideal rate of tax, T^1, where tax revenue will be maximised. Individuals will not feel the need to decrease their work or find ways of avoiding paying tax, tax avoidance.

The policy implication is that if a country's tax rate is at T^2 and it is reduced to T^1, then tax revenue will actually increase. This reasoning has formed the basis of the tax changes that have occured in the UK since 1979.

16 The national debt

When governments fail to cover all their expenditure from taxation they finance the deficit by borrowing. The cumulative total of outstanding debts owed by successive governments is referred to as the **national debt**. The major part of the debt is in the form of different government securities some of which is long term debt and some short term. Much of the debt is held by institutions such as banks, insurance companies and pension funds, and much of the debt is marketable in that it can be bought and sold on secondary markets such as the stock exchange and the money market. The debt has tended to grow most rapidly during wars when it is impossible for governments to finance all of their expenditure from taxation. Growth of the debt is not in itself a bad thing provided its growth rate is not significantly faster than the rate of growth of gross domestic product.

Self assessment questions

1 State the four principles of taxation.
2 Distinguish between direct and indirect taxation.
3 Distinguish between regressive and progressive taxation.
4 Why is progressive taxation considered to be more equitable than proportionate taxation?
5 What is the national debt?
6 How does the unemployment trap arise and how would a negative income tax system attempt to overcome the situation?

8

The banking system and the control of credit

In this chapter we will discuss the structure of the UK banking system, the role of the Bank of England, the process by which the commercial banks can create credit and the way in which this credit creating ability is controlled by the Bank of England.

1 The Bank of England

The Bank of England (referred to as 'The Bank') is the institution in the UK which is vested with the control of the banking system and, jointly with the Treasury, the implementation of the government's monetary policy. Banks which undertake these responsibilities are referred to as **central banks** or **reserve banks** and are found in most industrialised countries.

Since its founding in 1694 the Bank of England has always been closely associated with government policy, a fact which was explicitly recognised when it was taken into public ownership in 1946.The Bank is managed by a board of directors, known as the Court, which consists of a governor, deputy governor and 16 directors, all appointed by the crown. For accounting purposes the Bank is divided into two functions each producing its own balance sheet.

- **The Issue Department** is responsible for the notes in circulation and their issue.
- **The Banking Department** is responsible for the other functions of the Bank of England and the commercial banks.

2 The Bank Charter Act

The **Bank Charter Act of 1844** allowed the note issue to exceed the stock of gold backing the issue. Notes not backed by gold are known as the **fiduciary issue**. Since 1931 when the 'Gold Standard' was abandoned, the whole of the note issue has been fiduciary. It is no longer backed by gold and neither is it convertible into gold, its backing now being confidence in its value.

3 The Bank's traditional responsibilities

The responsibilities of the Bank of England can be summarised as follows:

- It acts as banker to the government, and as such it keeps the accounts of the government departments. In order to ensure that the government always has sufficient finance for its expenditure it manages the government's short term borrowing requirement through the Treasury Bill issue and by making advances. It also manages the longer term debt of the public sector, maintains the stock register, pays dividends, and conducts new issues.
- It is also responsible for providing financial advice to the government.
- It is responsible, together with the Treasury, for implementing the government's monetary policy.
- It is the 'bankers' bank'. The commercial banks maintain their balances in current accounts with the Bank. It also provides them with advice and assistance.
- The Bank is the sole authority responsible for issuing notes in England and Wales.
- The Bank acts on behalf of the government on the foreign exchange market when intervention is felt to be necessary to support the pound.
- It acts as 'lender of last resort' to the banking system. If there is a problem of liquidity in the banking system the Bank will give assistance.
- The Bank participates in the activities of such international agencies as the International Monetary Fund and the International Bank for Reconstruction and Development (IBRD).
- The Bank also acts as banker to foreign central banks.
- An important role is the supervising of the banking and financial institutions in order to ensure their stability and efficient operation. When part of the system is in difficulty the Bank will provide support so as to prevent any undermining of the stability of the system as a whole. The major institutions take advice and leadership from the Bank partly because of its pre-eminent role in the system, but also because in the final analysis it may be essential to their survival. The fall of BCCI saw the Bank of England investigating and producing new guidelines for all banking and financial institutions.

4 Changes in financial supervision

May 1997 saw the biggest overhaul of financial supervision for many decades.

The newly elected Labour government changed two major aspects of the Bank of England's responsibilities.

- The Bank was given sole responsibility for the rate of interest, the Bank Rate, without government interference.
- The supervisory function of the Bank was removed with the intention of setting up a

new 'super-regulator'. This body would combine the functions of all of the previous supervisory bodies such as the SIB, PIA etc.

5 The money market

The **money market** is a general term used for a variety of financial institutions and includes:

- Discount houses
- Commercial banks
- Merchant banks (also known as 'accepting houses').
- The foreign exchange market.

6 The discount market

The discount market comprises of the eleven institutions which are members of the London Discount Market Association (LDMA). The original function of discount houses was to provide cash immediately, less a discount, to holders of bills of exchange which were not due for payment until after three months or longer. The discount houses are now recognised as occupying a central role in the financial system. They act in an intermediary role between the Bank of England and the commercial banks. The Bank of England utilises the discount market to implement its money market operations as part of its overall monetary policy.

To the commercial banks the discount market provides a form of investment which has the two desirable characteristics of being both **highly liquid** (i.e. can easily and quickly be repaid), and **safe.** Because the commercial banks can call in this money at very short notice it is referred to as **money at call.** The discount houses use these funds to invest in short-term assets such as Treasury bills and commercial bills.

Should the discount houses find themselves short of funds, for example if the banks call in their investments, then the discount houses can borrow from the Bank of England against suitable collateral. Because the terms of such lending, such as interest rates and duration of the loan, are so severe, the Bank of England is referred to as the **lender of last resort.** These stringent conditions are imposed because the arrangement is not intended to be part of the everyday operations of the Bank of England but as a true last resort.

This last resort borrowing facility is extended only to the discount houses. In return for this privilege the discount houses are expected to tender (offer to buy) each week the full issue of Treasury bills on offer. Normally other institutions will also want to buy them so the discount houses will only be required to buy a part of the issue, but in the event of there being a deficiency of demand the government can be assured that all the issue will be taken up and can therefore be certain of meeting its short-term borrowing requirement.

The Bank of England does not deal directly with the commercial banks, and the discount houses play an intermediary role between them. The Bank of England does not lend directly to the banks but does lend to, or buy bills from, the discount houses. In this way the Bank of England increases the stock of balances at the central bank which is available to the commercial banks. If the commercial banks run short of balances they call in their 'money at call' from the discount houses. These funds have however been reinvested in various short term assets and in order to meet their commitments the discount houses will be forced to utilise the services of the 'lender of last resort' – the Bank of England. By borrowing from the Bank of England the discount houses pass on these central bank balances to the commercial banks. The discount houses could be said to act as a 'buffer' between the Bank of England and the banking system.

7 Authorised institutions

Following the **1987 Banking Act** any institution wishing to carry on a banking role now requires to be authorised by the Bank of England. These banks, known as **Authorised Institutions,** are expected to provide information to the Bank on a regular basis and to respond to directives when given. The Bank also lays down criteria for the capital adequacy of the Institutions. The Act provides legal support to the supervisory role of the Bank of England over the banking system.

8 Treasury bills

Treasury bills are issued each week by the Bank of England on behalf of the government and are one of the means by which the government covers its short term borrowing requirement. The amounts vary between £5,000 and £1 million and are normally issued for a period of 91 days after which they are redeemable.

9 Government stocks (gilts)

The government also raises revenue through the sale of longer dated (or undated) securities. These are sold by the Bank's broker on the securities market, and as they are less liquid than Treasury bills they tend to be purchased outside the banking sector as well as within it. Government stocks can be bought and sold also on the secondary market (i.e. retraded after being acquired) and as they carry a fixed rate of interest the yield will vary inversely with the price.

10 Retail banks

Retail banks are those banks offering retail banking services to both the business and personal sector through a branch network. The main feature of these commercial banks is the money transmission function through cheques etc. The settlement of drawings by cheque or by other means is carried out through the banks Clearing House or banks Automated Clearing Services.The retail banks at January 1991 were:
Allied Irish Banks plc.; Bank of England, Banking Department; Bank of Ireland; Bank of Scotland; Barclays; Clydesdale; Co-operative; Coutts and Co.; Girobank; Lloyds; Midland; National Westminster; Northern Bank; Royal Bank of Scotland; TSB; Ulster Bank; Yorkshire Bank.

Much inter-bank indebtedness is self cancelling. For example, many of the cheques drawn on Barclays by Lloyds can be offset against cheques drawn on Lloyds by Barclays. This offsetting is carried out by the Clearing House and at the end of the day only the net indebtedness which is left is adjusted through the commercial banks' current accounts at the Bank of England.

11 Functions of commercial banks

One of the main functions of the commercial banks is to accept the deposits of their customers. Deposits can be held in one of three, ways:

- **Current accounts (sight deposits)**: These accounts do not earn interest and may be subject to charges for transactions. They are normally held for their convenience as a means of payment by cheque and they can be withdrawn on demand.
- **Deposit accounts (time deposits)**: These accounts earn interest and cannot be transferred by cheque. For large withdrawals a period of notice may be required, although today most banks show a degree of flexibility over this.
- **Large deposits:** Larger deposits attract a higher rate of interest. For deposits of about £50,000 or more a **certificate of deposit (CD)** may be issued. These have a maturity of between 3 months and 5 years and as they are **negotiable instruments** they can be traded. The banks find them a useful means of raising large sums of money for fixed periods; holders of CD's find them useful as they can be sold if funds are required immediately.

12 Liquidity v profit

Commercial banks like all companies need to earn a profit for their shareholders. This requirement however creates a dilemma for banking operations. Banks also have obligations to their depositors to pay them upon demand and to safeguard their deposits. When a customer makes a deposit with a commercial bank that deposit will be reinvested either in loans or on the money market, or elsewhere; but what is important is that the customers believe their deposits are safe. If customers collectively feared for the safety of their deposits and demanded them all back at the same time the bank would be unable to pay them out and in the absence of assistance from the central bank, may collapse. This is referred to as a 'run on the bank' and was common during the recession in the USA during the late 1920's. In order to be able to pay on demand the banks need to maintain a percentage of their total deposits in the form of cash (the cash ratio) and some in the form of assets which are easy to liquidate ('money at call'). The commercial banks have found that they can operate effectively on a cash ratio of about 8% which is sufficient to meet the everyday demands for cash. The desire to make profit, however, conflicts with the need to maintain liquidity in a system based almost entirely upon confidence, as the more profitable investments tend to be less liquid. Also profits are higher the more risky the investment, but a high level of risk may result in a loss of confidence. The art of successful banking is therefore to maintain a balanced 'portfolio' of investments. Bank investments therefore contain a range of investments from very low to modest risk, and with varying degrees of liquidity. Table 8.1 lists the assets held by the London clearing banks (May, 1995).

Prior to 1971 the banks were required to maintain 28% of their assets in investments which were highly liquid, this was referred to as the 'liquidity ratio', and included an 8% cash ratio; both of which were abandoned in 1971. For operating purposes however banks still require a cash ratio and some of their assets in investments which are easy to liquidate. Because of the large proportion of transactions which are now carried out by cheque the banks tend to maintain a smaller cash ratio, as can be seen from Table 8.1

TABLE 8.1

The Sterling assets of the London clearing banks (May 1995)

	£mn	Per cent
Notes and coin	3,620	0.05
Balances with the Bank of England	1,571	0.23
Treasury Bills	9,424	1.39
Other bills	14,013	2.08
Money at call with the London discount market	6,474	0.96
Other market loans	175,075	25.8
Advances	405,120	59.87
Banking department lending to central government	1,581	0.23
British government stocks	15,616	2.30
Other investments	44,104	6.52
	676,688	

13 Credit creation

Banks have a powerful ability to **create credit,** and as credit can be considered as a form of money in that it facilitates the purchase of goods, governments need to exert some degree of control over this credit creating ability.

This ability to create credit arises from the fact stated above, that the banks only require a small fraction of their total deposits in the form of cash; just sufficient to meet the daily demands of their customers. This cash ratio is generally a percentage of total deposits and for purposes of illustration we will assume it is 10% (although in reality it could be much smaller). With a cash ratio of 10% a deposit of £50 would be used as the basis for creating £450 in credit money (i.e. £50 is 10% of £500 and £450 + £50 = £500). This is made possible by the fact that when a bank makes an advance to a customer the customer's account is credited and he will then probably use a cheque to obtain the goods he requires, the recipient of the cheque will then redeposit the cheque into the banking system, which because of the operation of the clearing system has a similar effect to that of redepositing the cheque with the same bank. In Figure 8.1, 'A' has deposited £50 with his bank. With a cash ratio of 10% the bank creates credit for 'C' by crediting his account with £450. 'C' uses this to buy goods for £200 from 'D' and £250 from 'E', paying them both by cheque. These cheques are eventually redeposited with the bank, and even if 'E' and 'D' draw some cash, statistically it will be unlikely to be of such an amount that it could not be met from the £50 initial deposit and still leave sufficient for the average cash demand of 'A'. As stated earlier it does not matter if the cheques are deposited with a different bank because of the clearing arrangements, and as they do not draw cash against each other they operate in a similar manner to a single bank.

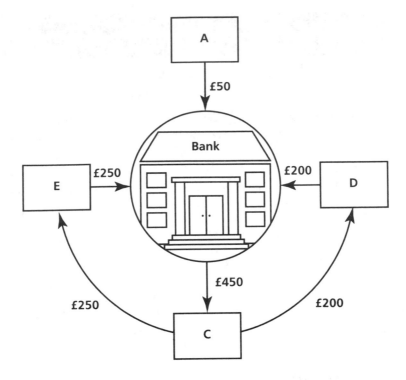

Figure 8.1

14 Credit multiplier

The process of credit creation is referred to as the **bank credit multiplier**. In order to explain this process further it is necessary to appreciate that a cardinal rule of banking is that they must maintain an **equality between their assets and liabilities** on their balance sheets. It should also be noted that as far as a bank is concerned **deposits** appear as a **liability** on the balance sheets as they have a liability to repay the customer, and **advances** (loans) appear as **assets.**

In order to simplify the explanation of the process of credit creation we will assume initially that the economy's banking system consists of a single bank only. Because of this all credit, also referred to as **created deposits**, will be deposited with the same bank. If we also assume a 10% cash ratio for ease of calculation we can illustrate the process in Table 36.2.

TABLE 8.2				
	LIABILITIES (£)		ASSETS (£)	
Period I	Initial deposits	25,000	Notes and coin	25,000
Period 2	Initial deposits	25,000	Notes and coin	25,000
	Created deposits	<u>225,000</u>	Loans (credit)	<u>225,000</u>
		250,000		250,000

In period 1 the bank has attracted initial deposits from its customers of £25,000. Operating on a cash ratio of 10%, which is considered to be sufficient to meet the average withdrawal, then loans can be advanced to the extent of £225,000 (9 × 25,000). These loans will eventually be spent, probably by cheque, and as we have assumed a single bank they will be redeposited with the same bank, and in period 2 they then show on the liabilities side of the balance sheet in the form of **created deposits.** It should be noted that initial deposits of £25,000 have served to create credit nine times greater (£225,000). This **multiple expansion of credit** is also referred to as the **bank credit multiplier**.

Dropping the assumption of a single bank economy makes little difference to the ability to create credit. In a multi-bank system such as the UK the only difference is that the initial cash deposits are divided between the various banks, but assuming the same cash ratio is maintained the same **total** amount of credit will be created. Even if the different banks were not equally successful in attracting deposits only the final distribution will be affected and not the total amount of credit. As mentioned above, although we have a multi-bank system it operates in a similar manner to a single bank system through the operation of the clearing system.

15 Limits to credit creation

The ability of the banks to create credit is powerful, but not unlimited. Limitations to credit creation are as follows:

- An over extension of credit would increase the proportion of bad debts which would undermine both profitability and confidence.
- The need to maintain liquidity in a system where confidence is paramount.
- Controls exerted over the banks by the Bank of England as part of the government's monetary policy (see Chapter 11).

16 The principles of banking

The principles of sound banking can be summarised as:

- The balancing of profit and risk so as to maintain confidence and at the same time produce an adequate return.
- Maintain confidence by demonstrating both integrity and soundness.
- To maintain adequate liquid assets in order to ensure that withdrawals can be met.
- To ensure that assets are equal to liabilities on the balance sheet.

Self assessment questions

1 What are the main functions of the Bank of England at present?
2 What role does the discount market play in the financial structure?
3 Describe the function of the bankers' clearing house.
4 Outline the process by which banks can bring about the multiple expansion of credit.
5 What are the principles of sound banking?
6 What are the characteristics of a liquid asset?
7 To what extent do balance sheets of commercial banks reflect their function?

9

Inflation

1 A definition

Inflation refers to a **generalised and sustained rise in the price level**, or a **fall in the value of money,** both of which amount to the same thing - that a unit of currency will buy fewer goods. Inflation does not refer to the fact that some goods have become more expensive than others because **relative prices** change constantly according to demand and supply. Inflation refers to the fact that the price of **all** goods is rising.

2 The retail price index

It is not merely the fact that prices are rising which is important but rather the **rate of increase**. This is usually stated as the **annual rate of inflation** as measured by a **price index,** the most frequently quoted index of inflation is the **retail price index**. There are also manufacturing and wholesale price indices but the retail price index measures inflation as it affects the majority of people. The index is constructed from price data gathered in the **family expenditure survey** and is constructed from the prices of a collection of goods and services which enter a typical shopping 'basket', each item being weighted in accordance with its importance in the household budget. The 'basket of goods' is then revalued in each subsequent year at current prices, and inflation is represented by the increase in the index. The composition of the basket is changed periodically to keep abreast of changes in expenditure patterns. The index becomes outdated in its coverage eventually as the year upon which it was based becomes more distant in time. A further weakness is that during periods of rapid inflation the index may exaggerate inflation as consumers substitute those goods which are rising less rapidly in price and therefore become relatively cheaper. Index numbers represent percentage changes rather than absolute changes. For example in the base year the index will be 100; if in the following year the index is 120 then the index has risen by 20 percentage points. (See Appendix).

3 Real and nominal values

When comparing economic statistics over time it is necessary to **deflate** the data in order to eliminate the effect of inflation. For example, if incomes rise by 20% over a year but prices have risen by 15% the **real** increase in incomes is approx. 5% (actually 4.4%).

Money (or **nominal**) incomes (or wages) refers to income in terms of the number of pounds earned. **Real** incomes (or wages) refers to the actual increase in purchasing power after allowing for the effects of inflation.

$$\frac{\text{monetary income}}{\text{RPI}} \times 100 = \text{real income}$$

Increases in income may appear far more modest after allowing for the effects of inflation.

4 GDP deflator

It is also necessary to deflate the data when comparing GDP over different time periods in order to estimate the rate of growth of the economy. This is achieved in a similar manner to above by the use of the **implied deflator** for GDP. This is obtained by dividing the value of GDP at current prices by GDP at constant (1990) prices.

$$\frac{\text{GDP (nominal)}}{\text{GDP (1990 prices)}} = \text{GDP at constant prices}$$

5 Inflation trends

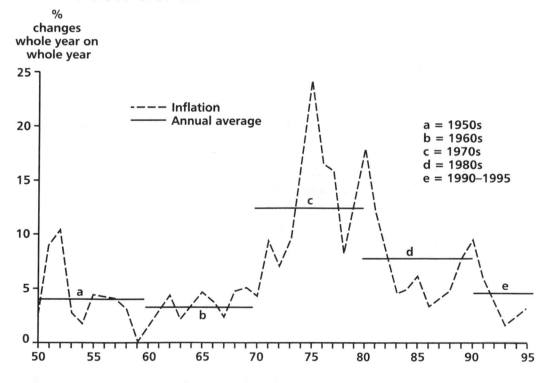

Figure 9.1 UK inflation 1950–95

Slow rates of inflation of 2–3% will always be present in a growing economy and may even be conducive to growth itself. When inflation rises to very high levels however the effects can be very damaging on the economy and is therefore unacceptable to most governments.

Sustained high rates of inflation, known as **hyperinflation**, have occurred several times in history, in particular the German inflation of 1923 and the Hungarian inflation of 1944. In Britain the 1970s saw higher rates of inflation than any other period in the twentieth century. Retail prices rose on average by 12.4% per annum between 1970 and 1979, compared with 3.5% between 1960 and 1969. Inflation in Britain reached a peak of 24% in 1975 before declining to an average of around 7% in the 1980s and 4% in the 1990s. Figure 9.1 illustrates the recent trends in inflation.

Although high rates of inflation are considered to be undesirable and most governments give priority to controlling it there are examples of countries enduring very high rates of inflation over sustained periods, in particular South American countries such as Chile and Brazil, but often only at the cost of foregoing democratic freedoms, and abject poverty for a large section of the population.

6 Causes

The causes of inflation are the subject of much controversy and academic debate, some of which will be discussed later; it is however common practice to classify inflation into two categories: demand-pull inflation and cost-push inflation.

7 Demand-pull inflation

Demand-pull inflation is defined as a situation where **aggregate demand exceeds aggregate supply at current prices,** hence prices are 'pulled up' by the total demand for goods and services exceeding what the economy is capable of producing. Inflation of this type is associated with the full employment of resources, where there is spare capacity of either, or, both labour and capital, an increase in demand may be achieved without a significant rise in the price level. If resources are fully utilised however it will not be possible in the short run to meet any increase in demand by increasing output and the excess demand can only result in an increase in the price level. An example of demand-pull inflation occurred during the Korean War (1950/51) when the western world was unwilling to forego its current consumption of goods following the austerity years after World War II but the western governments were engaged in a conflict in Korea which was demanding a high level of resource consumption. World demand for resources exceeded what could be supplied and prices rose substantially. Attempting to achieve high rates of economic growth during a period of full employment may also result in excess demand and rising prices.

8 Cost-push inflation

Cost-push inflation is a consequence of rising costs which tend to push up prices. It is **not** a consequence of excess demand for goods resulting in increased demand for factors, higher factor prices and therefore higher prices to the consumer. Cost-push inflation occurs when costs rise independently of an increase in demand. Cost inflation can result from some, or all, of the following:

- Increases in wages which are greater than the increase in productivity.
- A fall in the exchange rate which increases the cost of imported materials.
- A rise in the cost of imported materials due to other factors abroad, for example the

formation of the OPEC cartel and its effect on oil prices in the 1970s.
- Increases in indirect taxation (i.e. taxes on goods and services such as VAT).

Entrepreneurs tend to have a fairly fixed idea of the sort of profit margins they should be making, and as the costs of production rise they attempt to maintain these margins by marking up prices to the consumer.

9 Expectations

Expectations play an important role in the inflationary process. As inflation is experienced over a period of time employees tend to start thinking in terms of real wages rather than nominal (money) wages, i.e. they see through the 'veil of money', and begin to anticipate inflation. As a result union negotiators start to build a 'hedge' against inflation into wage negotiations. So, for example, if the union wants to gain a 10% increase in real wages for its members and anticipated inflation is 15%, and assuming 5% will be given away during the bargaining process, the union will bargain initially for a 30% increase:

> **30% (Union claim)**
> **– 5% Lost during negotiation**
> **– 15% Lost due to inflation**
> **= 10% Increase in real wages**

10 Sustained inflation

If we consider the causes of demand-pull and cost-push inflation we can see quite easily why they may result in a rise in the price level. They do not explain however how they can generate a sustained and generalised rise in the price level over a period of time, rather than a once-and-for-all increase. If however, we combine them with the effects of the expectations described above, and extend the effects to include the exchange rate and overseas trade we can see how a rise in the price level can start a **wage/price spiral**, resulting in a sustained period of inflation. Such a process is outlined in Figure 9.2 and it should be noted that in the example the process begins with a period of demand-pull inflation which becomes transformed into cost-push inflation, but the process could start just as easily with cost-push inflation.

11 Incomes policies

Keynesians (after J. M. Keynes, see Chapter 12) see costs as being the main determinants of prices and the most important element in costs is considered to be wages. They therefore suggest that the best way to control inflation is to control wages. Wage controls, such as the various **incomes policies** which were pursued in the 1960s and 1970s, should therefore be imposed at point A in Figure 9.2 to keep the wage increases at or below the rate of increase of productivity. Such policies can be either:

- Voluntary
- Statutory

The results of such policies are however inconclusive and their effects on inflation appear to be only temporary.

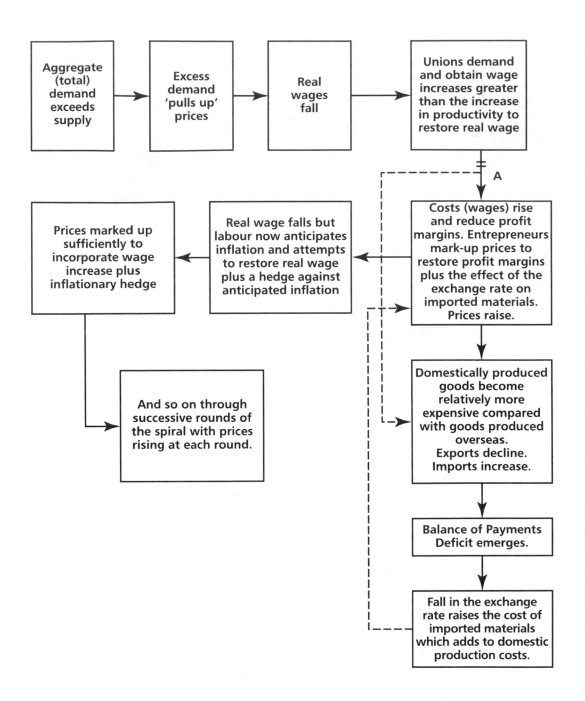

Figure 9.2

12 Monetarists view

Monetarists consider that inflation is due solely to the over expansion of the money supply by governments and that attempts to control inflation by any means other than the strict control of the money supply will be doomed to failure (see Chapter 16 for further details).

13 The quantity theory of money

The quantity theory of money attempts to explain the relationship between the supply of money and the price level. In its most basic form it can be expressed as

$$MV = PT$$

where

M = the money supply, or stock
V = the velocity of circulation of money
P = the price level
T = the volume of transactions

The left hand side of the equation represents the total amount of money used to finance transactions in a given period and the right hand side total expenditures in that period. Both sides are therefore equal. Because velocity (V) is a residual, calculated as PT/M, and is included to make both sides of the equation balance, the equation is sometimes referred to as a tautology (self evident). It is still useful however in identifying the variables which influence the value of money. Classical economic theory assumed that both V and T would be constant in the short run. Any change in the money supply (M) would therefore have an equal effect on the price level (P).

ie
$$M\bar{V} = P\bar{T}$$

If there were a substantial reserve of unemployed resources however an increase in M, with V remaining constant would result in increased output and therefore transactions, with P remaining unchanged.

There is much controversy however over whether or not V is in fact constant. If V varies then it is quite conceivable that an increase in M could be offset by a reduction in V leaving the price level (P) unchanged. During deep recessions such as that of the 1930s, spending was greatly reduced, which did in fact result in a reduction in V. During periods of hyper-inflation one of the characteristics is a rapid increase in V as people spend their cash balances as quickly as possible before they lose their value. More recent adaptations of the quantity theory will be discussed in the chapter on monetarism (Chapter 16).

14 Purchasing power parity

In an open economy such as Britain's it is not possible to isolate the domestic inflation rate from inflation in the rest of the world and inflation can be transmitted through the relative exchange rates. This is the **purchasing power parity** theory which holds true in the long run although there may be deviations from it in the short run. There is therefore a transmission mechanism through which inflation can become internationally transmitted. It should be noted in this context that the high rate of inflation of the 1970s was by no means restricted to Britain but also appeared in most industrialised countries.

15 The evils of inflations

Inflation is generally considered to be undesirable for the following reasons:

- The longer debtors can delay repayment of debts the less they repay in real terms, therefore debtors gain and creditors lose and eventually there is a reluctance to give credit. As credit is the basis of trade, inflation eventually results in a breakdown of trading relationships.
- The reluctance to give credit results in higher interest rates.
- There is an arbitrary income redistribution between groups in society. Those on fixed incomes, non union labour, and weaker groups generally lose out to well organised, stronger groups or those who set their own incomes through commission or profits.
- The value of savings is rapidly eroded leaving the saving classes embittered.
- The dangers from inflation are by no means all economic and possibly the greatest problems of inflation arise from the social and political strains it places upon society, in particular its divisiveness between different groups within society. For these reasons most democratic governments give high priority in their economic policies to curbing it.

APPENDIX

The construction of retail price index

| Item | Weights | Year 1 (Y1) | | | Year 2 (Y2) | | |
		Price	Base year index	Weighted price index	Price	Index Y2 as a % of Y1	Weighted price index
Potatoes	5	10p	100	500	15p	150	750
Milk	3	30p	100	300	39p	130	390
Meat	2	£1.50	100	200	£1.65	110	220
	10			1000÷10			1360÷10
		Base year index =		100	Year 2 index =		136
				YEAR 1 = 100			
				YEAR 2 = 136			

An increase in the retail price index of 36 percentage points.

STAGES

1 Select appropriate weights reflecting the importance of the item in the household budget.
2 Set base year index = 100. weights × index = weighted price index. The sum of the weighted price index ÷ the sum of the weights = base year index.
3 Second year index calculated as year 2 prices as a percentage of year 1 prices.
4 Year 2 weighted price index = Year 2 index × weight.
5 Year 2 index = the sum of the weighted price index ÷ the sum of the weights.
6 The procedure is continued in a similar manner for each subsequent year.

Index numbers can be used to 'deflate' data for purposes of making comparisons over time. Deflating data removes the effects of inflation so comparisons can be made in real terms. The technique is often used to make comparisons of gross domestic product over a time period, or the growth of incomes.

e.g. Real weekly earnings for 1992 at Jan. '84 prices $= \dfrac{£230.00}{32.4} \times 100 = £71.78$

The data above shows that weekly earnings have risen faster than prices in every year except 1986 when 'real' weekly earnings fell. However, the increase in income is much lower in real terms than in nominal, or money, terms.

EXAMPLE:

Year	Average Weekly Earnings(£)	Retail Price Index	'Real' weekly earnings at Jan. ' 84 prices
1984	65.75	100	65.75
1986	95.90	157.1	61.04
1988	130.00	197.1	65.96
1990	180.00	263.7	68.26
1992	230.00	320.4	71.78

Self assessment questions

1 Distinguish between cost-push and demand-pull inflation.

2 Outline what is meant by a 'wage price spiral'.

3 State the quantity theory of money and outline how it relates the money supply to the price level.

4 How is inflation measured?

5 Explain the role of expectations in generating wage inflation.

6 Why is inflation considered to be undesirable?

10

Defining the money supply

Before we consider the policy instruments which may be utilised by government in the control of the money supply (Chapter 11) we need to define precisely what we mean by the money supply.

1 A definition

Money can be defined as anything which is generally acceptable in return for goods and services, however in an advanced economy such a definition is not sufficiently precise for operational purposes. The main definitions used in the UK are M0 and M4. M0 is generally referred to as a 'narrow' definition of money and M4 as a 'broad' definition. The components of these definitions are approximately as follows:

- M0 = Notes and coins in circulation with the public + banks' till money + banks' operational balances with the Bank of England.
- M4 = Notes and coins in circulation with the public + private sector sterling time bank deposits + building society deposits.

(Note that sight bank deposits are generally referred to as current accounts and time deposits as deposit accounts).

Prior to 1987 the main definitions in use were M0, Ml, sterling M3 (£M3) and the measures of private sector liquidity PSLI and PSL2. The main measure for targeting purposes between 1976 and 1987 was £M3, but the targeting of £M3 was abandoned because it was always outside the growth range targeted and also its relationship to money GDP was never clear. In March 1987 two new broad definitions were introduced M4, and M5 as a new measure of private sector liquidity. The exact composition of the main monetary aggregates is given in Figure 10.1.

Main monetary aggregates
Narrow money 'Narrow money' refers to money balances which are readily available to finance current spending, that is to say for 'transactions purposes'.
M0 Notes and coin in circulation with the public plus banks' till money plus banks' operational balances with the Bank of England
Broad money 'Broad money' refers to money held for transactions purposes and money held as a form of saving. It provides an indicator of the private sector's holdings of relatively liquid assets – assets which could be converted with relative ease and without capital loss into spending on goods and services.
M3 Notes and coin in circulation with the public plus private sector sterling sight bank deposits plus private sector sterling time bank deposits plus private sector holdings of sterling bank certificates of deposit
M4 M3 plus private sector holdings of building society shares and deposits and sterling certificates of deposit minus building society holdings of bank deposits and bank certificates of deposit, and notes and coin
M5 M4 plus holdings by the private sector (excluding building societies) of money market instruments (bank bills, Treasury bills, local authority deposits), certificates of tax deposit and national savings instruments (excluding certificates, SAYE and other long-term deposits)

Figure 10.1
Source: EPR No 195

2 Money aggregates

The definitions above are often referred to as monetary 'aggregates' as they aggregate together various forms of 'money'.

- **Narrow money** refers generally to money held predominantly for spending immediately or in the near future on goods and services, i.e. for transactions purposes.
- **Broad money** refers generally to money held for transactions purposes and as a store of value. When we say that it provides a guide to liquidity, we mean that it provides an indicator of the private sectors' holding of relatively liquid assets – i.e. assets which could be converted with relative ease into spending on goods and services without capital loss.

3 Changing measures

It would appear that the introduction of M0 in March 1984 was a consequence of the difficulty in achieving targets for monetary growth utilising broader definitions such as M3. Broad measures give an indication of the growth of liquidity in the economy whilst narrower definitions give a better idea of how money is being used for transactions as opposed to saving.

Because of institutional changes which take place in the economy it becomes necessary to adjust the definitions, particularly the broader ones, from time to time. The introduction of M4 in May 1987 reflects the fact that the distinction between building societies and banks had become increasingly blurred and that building society deposits are increasingly used for transactions rather than just savings. Also the building societies now offer a wide range of banking services, such as cheque book facilities and cash points, and since the 1986 Building Societies Act they have been able to extend their lending beyond lending for house purchase and can grant loans and issue credit cards. At the same time the banks have greatly expanded their mortgage lending. The trend for building societies to become PLC's and gain full bank status has confused the situation even further. These developments make it sensible to concentrate on measures of broad money like M4 which include the liabilities of both banks and building societies rather than measures such as M3 which cover only those of the banks. M5 is a broad 'liquidity' aggregate and is an excellent measure of those assets which constitute a temporary abode of purchasing power. M4 has totally replaced £M3 as the main focus of attention in terms of broad money.

4 A summary

Narrow and broad definitions can be summarised as:

Narrow = M0
Broad = M3, M4, M5.

The composition of the main monetary definitions is summarised in Figure 10.2

5 The PSBR

The **public sector borrowing requirement (PSBR)** refers to the deficit between the income and expenditure of the public sector (in particular central and local government). It arises because governments have generally failed to balance their budgets (see Chapter 12) i.e. their expenditures have been greater than their incomes from taxation and other sources. This deficit is usually financed by debt sales (government bonds etc.) to the 'non bank' private sector, borrowing from the banking system, borrowing from overseas, or by issuing more cash (notes and coin) to the public. There is a close relationship between the PSBR and the money supply, which will be explored more closely in Chapter 16.

6 Control of the money supply

If we consider, for the purposes of our discussion, control of the money supply to refer to the M4 definition, we can identify those variables for which policies will be required in the control of the money supply:

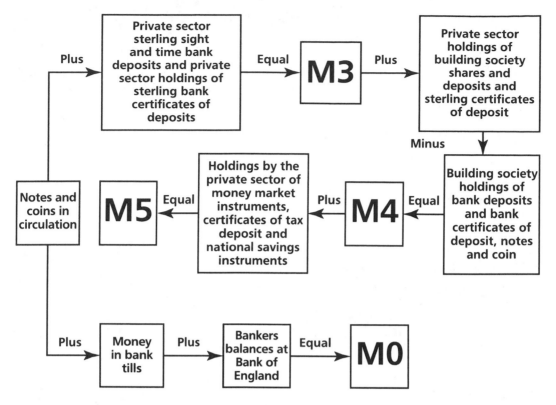

Figure 10.2 Composition of the main monetary aggregates

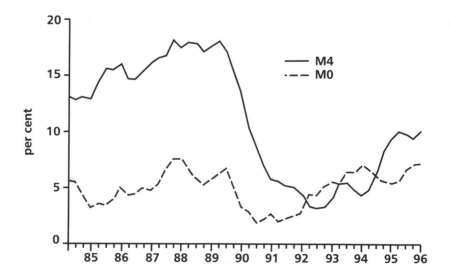

Figure 10.3 Broad and narrow money growth 1980–1996

- Bank lending to the private sector (credit policy).
- The control of the size of the PSBR.
- The sale of more public sector debt to the non-banks (debt management policy).

In the UK, between 1987 and 1990, public sector income exceeded expenditure, this budget surplus is referred to as public sector debt repayment (PSDR) as it is available for repayment of the national debt.

Self assessment questions

1 Distinguish between 'broad' and 'narrow' definitions of money.

2 Define M0, M3 and M4.

3 What are the components of an increase in M4?

11

Instruments of monetary policy

1 Control of credit money

From our previous discussion it is evident that one of the main components of the money supply is credit money. If the government is to control the money supply it is therefore essential that it has some means of controlling the ability of the commercial banks to create credit.

In the period prior to 1971 credit creation was controlled in two ways:

- **Direct controls**. Direct controls were either of the **quantitative** type or the **qualitative** type.
  - **Quantitative controls** took the form of **ceilings** on the amount of credit which the main banks could create, and on hire purchase terms.
  - **Qualitative controls** were instructions regarding the composition of bank lending, i.e. those sectors of the economy to which the banks could lend, for example, preference to finance for exporters, or finance to be used for investment purposes.
- The other main instrument of control during this period was that the banks had to observe a 28% liquidity ratio, i.e. they had to hold a stock of specified liquid assets equal to 28% of their deposits, including an 8% cash ratio.

The main emphasis during this period was on direct controls.

2 Competition and credit control

In 1971 a new system of controls over credit creation was introduced, known as **Competition and Credit Control (CCC)**. These measures were intended to encourage greater competition in the monetary system and at the same time rely more heavily on market forces as a method of control, rather than direct controls. The new system of controls emphasised short term interest rates and the composition of the banks' balance sheets. The new regulations introduced a 12½% **reserve asset ratio** whereby all banks were to hold certain specified assets whose value was not to fall below 12% of their **eligible liabilities**. The **reserve assets** included:

- Balances with the Bank of England (other than special deposits).
- Treasury bills.
- Money at call with the London discount market.
- Gilt edged stock with less than a year to run to maturity
- Local authority and commercial bills eligible for rediscount at the Bank of England.

Most of these assets originate in the public sector and are therefore under the control of the Bank of England, and any reduction in their availability would mean that the banks would be forced to reduce the level of their deposits in order to maintain the 12½% ratio, and this would therefore restrict their ability to create credit. Some commentators suggest that the purpose of the 12 ½% ratio was primarily intended to ensure that banks continued to invest on the traditional money markets and that the fractional reserve aspect was intended to be of secondary importance, but this secondary role became increasingly prominent. These regulations were abandoned in August 1981.

3 Special deposits

Special deposits constituted a further instrument of control. These were first introduced in 1960 but became more important after the introduction of CCC. Special deposits are called in from the banks by the Bank of England and are held in a special account. While they are held by the Bank of England they do not form part of the banks' current assets (They are in fact 'frozen'). As these balances cannot be drawn upon like the commercial banks' normal Bank of England balances, they cannot be included as reserve assets. Special deposits therefore reduce the liquidity of the banks and in so doing restrict their ability to create credit.

4 Supplementary special deposits

By 1973 it became apparent that the level of interest rates was not in itself sufficient to control the growth of the money stock and in December 1973 an element of direct control was reintroduced in the form of the **supplementary special deposits scheme,** known generally as **'the corset'**. Under the scheme the Bank of England set a target rate of growth for each bank's interest bearing deposits. If the actual rate of growth of deposits exceeded the target rate a deposit had to be made in an account with the Bank of England. These deposits received no interest and grew progressively larger the more the banks exceeded the target growth rate for deposits. The effect of this 'corset' was similar to that of the ceilings imposed before 1971. The corset was however by-passed as credit was diverted into uncontrolled channels, a process referred to as 'disintermediation'; and also by the raising of funds through the issue of commercial bills – known as the 'bill leak'. The failure of the corset resulted in its abandonment in 1980, ordinary special deposits were however retained.

5 Open market operations

Open market operations are the means by which the Bank of England influences the stock of financial assets and thereby indirectly the lending of the banks. If the Bank of England's broker sells government securities on the market purchasers of these securities pay by cheques drawn on their banks in favour of the Bank of England. When these cheques are presented for payment the banks' deposits are reduced at the Bank of England. This reduces the liquid assets of the banks and to restore the ratio of assets to liabilities the banks are forced to reduce the amount of lending. When the Bank of England enters the market to purchase securities and pays for them with cheques drawn on itself it has the opposite effect as these cheques will be deposited in the sellers' bank accounts increasing the commercial banks' asset base and enabling them to create additional credit. To summarise:

- The **sale** of bonds **reduces** the money supply.
- The **purchase** of bonds **increases** the money supply.

6 Interest rate policy

Creating a reduction in liquidity by the use of open market operations also allowed the Bank of England to pursue its **interest rate policy**. In order to restore liquidity the banks would be forced to 'call in' money from the discount market (see Chapter 8). As the discount market would have this money invested in Treasury bills, bills of exchange and commercial loans, it may have to turn to the 'lender of the last resort' – the Bank of England. The rate at which the Bank of England was prepared to lend to the discount market was known as **minimum lending rate (MLR)**. An increase in MLR would reduce the profitability of the discount houses' operations and they would be forced to adjust their interest rates to restore their profitability, and all other interest rates, on bank loans, mortgages, hire purchase etc. would follow suit.

In 1981 however the Bank of England ceased declaring an official MLR but could still intervene to influence short-term interest rates. Control over short-term rates is now achieved by the Bank through its own market operations, by varying the supply of funds the general level of interest rates can be pushed up or down. The supply and demand for funds will determine the general level of interest rates whilst market forces are free to determine the pattern of interest rates between different institutions. The current objective of UK monetary policy is to keep inflation low and the Bank will raise short-term interest rates whenever it thinks inflation will rise significantly.

7 Funding

Funding operations refer to the practice of managing the government's debt in order to influence the money supply. These operations involve the replacing of maturing debts with longer-term securities in order to reduce the amount of liquidity in the economy, or vice versa to increase liquidity. A secondary consequence of such activities is ,however, to influence bond prices and therefore interest rates.

8 Abolition of CCC

Competition and credit control and its main provision the 12½% reserve asset ratio, was abandoned in August 1981 and was replaced by a new system of controls which were intended to give the government tighter control over the monetary aggregates (M0 and M4).

9 The 1981 monetary control arrangements

The main provisions of the new regulations introduced in August 1981 were as follows:

- All institutions in the monetary sector with eligible liabilities of over £10 million were required to hold ½% of eligible liabilities in non interest bearing balances at the Bank. The eligible reserve asset ratio and 1½% cash ratio were abolished. These new balances were intended to provide the Bank with the funds to conduct its open market operations.
- MLR was suspended. Money market operations were to be conducted with reference to a narrow band for short-term interest rates. MLR was however re-activated in January 1985 as a temporary measure in response to a sterling crisis. The purpose of this was to make indications of interest rate changes less visible and therefore less of a politically sensitive issue.
- Eligible banks were required to hold an average of 6% (now 5%) but never less than 4% (now 2½%) on a daily basis, of their eligible liabilities in secured money with the discount houses. This was intended to ensure that the traditional channels for such funds continued to be used.
- The Bank retained its function as 'lender of last resort' to the discount market but through the channels of open market operations.
- In order to give the Banks open market operations more impact and to widen the bill market, the number of eligible banks was increased.
- The banks were still to maintain their operational balances at the Bank for everyday clearances and also to enable the Bank to monitor the relationship between MO and the broad monetary aggregates.

The new arrangements introduced in 1981 meant that in future open market operations would operate solely upon the level of short-term interest rates and would allow more flexibility in interest rate policy. This implies that interest changes were considered to have importance as an instrument of money demand management. Short-term interest rates were to be determined by a combination of official influence and market forces. However under these new arrangements market forces would have the greater influence in the determination of short-term rates, whilst the Bank would influence only very short-term rates by its dealings with the discount market. Generally, however, interest rates were to be market determined.

The Bank's influence was to operate through an 'unpublished band of interest rates', which were essentially short term; by means of its dealings with the discount market. Should the Bank want to see a rise in short-term interest rates it would lend at a rate above market rates and because of its pre-eminent position in the money market this would tend to determine the short-term rate operating in that market. As discussed earlier, the relationship between interest rates and the money supply is complicated. However, despite this the Bank would still attempt to influence short-term rates because of their effect on the demand for credit, and therefore the money supply.

The three main policy instruments currently utilised for the control of the money stock are:

- **Fiscal policy** – controlling the supply of money through the reduction of the PSBR.
- **Funding** – sales of public sector debt to the non-bank private sector to offset the effects of the PSBR on the money supply.

- **Open market operations** – to influence short-term (and so long-term) interest rates and the demand for money.

Control of interest rates are now the main policy instrument by which government attempts to influence the demand for money.

10 Monetary growth targets

Since 1976 governments have followed the policy of announcing **targets** for the growth of the money stock, from 1976 to 1981 for M3 only, but in 1982 also for Ml and PSL2. In March 1984 the Treasury announced that monetary targets would be set for five years ahead rather than three as previously and would include a target for M0. Problems have been encountered in the past in achieving targets due to the difficulty of estimating the demand for bank lending; for example, other objectives were sometimes given priority over control of the money stock, and other factors which resulted in an increase in the stock of money, for example one of the main elements in the creation of money is the public sector borrowing requirement – was not under the direct control of the Bank of England. The persistent failure of the government to meet the target growth rates for the broad monetary aggregates has resulted in their abandonment and in the March 1988 budget a target growth rate for the narrow definition M0 only was announced. In 1993 the government specified a range for the annual growth of M4 of 3–9%. An outline of the way in which monetary targets have changed since 1980 is given in Appendix 1, Chapter 16.

Methods of monetary control have tended to reflect the prevailing attitude towards the importance of the role of money in the economy. In the era of the 1950's and.1960's following the Radcliffe Report money was not perceived as being a particularly important instrument of policy, but as this perception changed during the 1960's the money supply was seen as being increasingly important, a development which was reflected to a limited extent in the changes introduced in competition and credit control 1971. Throughout the 1970s, with the growing acceptance of the ideas of the 'monetarist' school of thought, money was viewed with growing importance and came to be seen by many as being the most important of economic variables; culminating in the 1981 monetary control arrangements.

Self assessment questions

1 Distinguish between qualitative and quantitative controls over bank lending.

2 What are special deposits?

3 What was the 12 ½ % reserve asset ratio introduced in the 1971 competition and credit control regulations?

4 How does the Bank of England utilise open market operations in order to influence the money supply?

5 How does the system of monetary controls introduced in 1981 operate?

12

The Keynesian model

1 The general theory

The idea that governments should attempt to manage the economy in order to achieve full employment owes much to J.M (Lord) Keynes. His book 'The General Theory of Employment Interest and Money' (1936) (referred to as 'The General Theory') was probably the most influential work on economics of the twentieth century and was used as the basis for managing the economies of the western world for the thirty years following 1945. This text attempts to do no more than explain in simple terms some of the ideas involved in the Keynesian model of demand management and it is recommended that you supplement it at a later stage with reading from a more advanced text.

2 Classical ideas

In order to understand Keynes' contribution it is useful to very briefly outline how economists before Keynes, referred to loosely as the 'classical economists', viewed the working of the economy. This is not an attempt to analyse the ideas of any particular economist but merely an overview of how the economy was considered to operate Classical economists believed that two essential principles prevailed:

- That the quantity theory of money operated (see Chapter 9).
- That Say's law of markets applied.

Say's law of markets is usually expressed as 'supply creates its own demand', or more literally that 'production creates the market for goods'. If these two principles are accepted it implies that the following points also apply:

- Prices and wages are flexible.
- Savings and investment are always brought into balance by movements in the interest rate, and all savings are therefore reinvested.

If we accept these principles then over-production of goods and unemployment become impossible, the economy will always tend towards equilibrium and by definition **equilibrium in the economy coincided with full employment**.

If we consider the process by which equilibrium was considered to be established, in very simple terms, we can see that prolonged periods of involuntary unemployment were not possible. In a situation where high unemployment did exist competition for jobs would depress wage rates until they became so low that entrepreneurs would take on additional labour. The very act of producing the extra output would, according to Say's law, generate sufficient purchasing power in the economy for its consumption. Also, according to the quantity theory, money balances were held only for making transactions.

It was not possible therefore for a situation of deficient total demand to exist. Savings could not exceed investment except in the short-run because the rate of interest would fall, deterring some saving whilst encouraging investment until they came into equilibrium, and vice versa if attempted investment exceeded savings.

The essential point was that in the absence of government intervention the economy would always tend back to the **full employment equilibrium**. Any unemployment which then existed was **voluntary** and occurred because workers were not willing to work at the prevailing market equilibrium wage rate.

3 Keynes' theory

The experience of the prolonged depression of the 1920s and 1930s and the failure of the economy to move automatically back to a situation of full employment caused Keynes to question the fundamental principles of the classical economists. Keynes argued that there was no longer an automatic tendency for the economy to move back to full employment because of changes which had taken place in the structure of the economy which made invalid some of the classical assumptions. In particular:

- Wages were no longer flexible in a downwards direction due to the growth of trade unions.
- The direct quantity theory relationship between money and prices was no longer valid.
- Saving and investment are carried out by distinctly different groups and there is no reason why what firms are **planning** to invest is necessarily the same as what they are **actually** able to invest. Also, what individuals are planning to save is not necessarily the same as what they actually manage to save. An increased desire to save by the whole community actually reduces consumption, and, therefore incomes, resulting in less actual saving (known as the **paradox of thrift**). It was possible therefore for **planned investment and savings to differ, and that equality between savings and investment is brought about not by changes in the interest rate but fluctuations in income and therefore employment**. As there was no tendency for the situation to change during the 1920s and 1930s the economy could be assumed to be in equilibrium **but with a high level of unemployment**. What Keynes argued was that a modern economy could be in equilibrium with **any** level of unemployment and stay there indefinitely. It was in fact **demand** which was deficient and the only way to achieve full employment was for the government to intervene and raise the level of demand thereby shifting the equilibrium point of the economy to coincide with the full employment level. Keynes' essential contribution was **the possibility of a less than full**

employment equilibrium, and the need for government intervention to manage the level of demand in order to achieve full employment.

4 The Keynesian model

Our initial analysis of the Keynesian model assumes that there is **no taxation or government activity, a closed economy (i.e. no imports or exports) and no changes in the price level.** As a consequence **all income** must be either **consumed** or **saved.** These simplifying assumptions will be dropped later.

5 The consumption function

The **consumption function** refers to the relationship between consumption (C) and income (Y). In the Keynesian model income is considered to be the most important determinant of consumption, i.e.

C = f(Y).

where f = function of, or depends upon, income

C = consumption
Y = income

If we drew a scatter diagram of an individual's consumption at different levels of income we would expect consumption to increase as income increases. This is illustrated in Figure 12.1 by the observations plotted on the diagram. A line of best fit drawn through the observations, i.e. C–C, is referred to as the **consumption function**. It can be observed that it is composed of a constant, a, and a slope or gradient, b, and if we assume a linear relationship (i.e. b is a constant) then the consumption function can be expressed as:

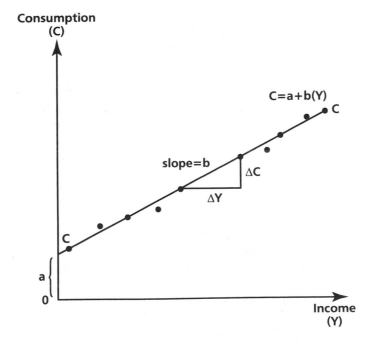

Figure 12.1

C = a + b(Y)

Where there are deductions from income in the form of taxation then consumption will depend upon the amount of **disposable income**, i.e.

C = a + b(Yd)

where Yd = disposable income.

6 The savings function

A 45° line drawn from the origin indicates the points where **consumption and income are exactly equal**. This is illustrated in Figure 12.2(a) where the 45° line has been superimposed onto the consumption function. At the equilibrium point E all income is consumed. Below E consumption exceeds income and there is 'dis-saving', for example, selling assets or living on earlier savings. Above E consumption is less than income and the area between CC and the 45° line represents savings. Ye is the equilibrium level of income. Figure 12.2(b) illustrates the **savings function** which corresponds with the pattern of con-

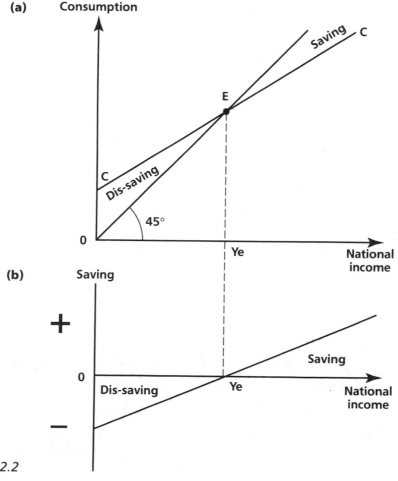

Figure 12.2

sumption and saving in 12.2(a). When income is below Ye saving is negative, and above Ye it is positive, and because of the relationship between consumption and saving both diagrams produce the same equilibrium level of income. Clearly it is **income** which determines **consumption** and **saving**.

7 The marginal propensity to consume and save

The marginal propensity to consume (MPC) refers to the amount of each additional unit of income which is consumed. It is calculated as:

$$\frac{\Delta C}{\Delta Y}$$

where C = consumption
Y = income
Δ = small change

It is the MPC which determines the shape of the consumption function, i.e. b in the formula C = a + b(Y).

The **marginal propensity** to save (MPS) refers to the amount of each additional increment of income which is saved. It is calculated as:

$$\frac{\Delta S}{\Delta Y}$$ where S = consumption

Because income can only be either consumed or saved then:

MPC + MPS = 1

8 APC and APS

The **average propensity to consume (APC)** and the **average propensity to save (APS)** refer to the distribution of **total** income between consumption and saving and can be calculated for **every** level of income. They are calculated as:

$$APC = \frac{C}{Y}$$

$$APS = \frac{S}{Y}$$

Table 12.1 illustrates the calculation of both the MPC and the APC.

TABLE 12.1				
Year	Income (Y)	Consumption (C)	MPC = $\Delta C/\Delta Y$	APC = C/Y
1996	1000	800		0.8
			150/200 = 0.75	
1998	1200	950		0.79

9 Total consumption

The consumption behaviour described so far referred to the individual, however by **aggregating each individual's consumption function** we can produce a similar consumption function for the economy as a whole relative to **national income**. There will also, therefore, be an MPC, MPS, APC and APS for the economy as a whole. From this point on therefore we will be referring to **total consumption (TC)** and **national income (Y)**.

10 National income equilibrium

Bearing in mind our assumptions regarding the closed economy and absence of government we can develop our conditions for national income equilibrium. In our analysis so far we have assumed that the only expenditure is consumption (C). However we know from our national income analysis that investment (I) is also an element in total expenditure. It is reasonable to assume that investment, like consumption, rises with income, therefore in Figure 12.3 an investment schedule (I) has been added. Aggregating the consumption and investment schedules produces the combined C + I schedule, to produce the equilibrium level of income Ye. In the lower Figure 12.3(b) this can be seen to be the

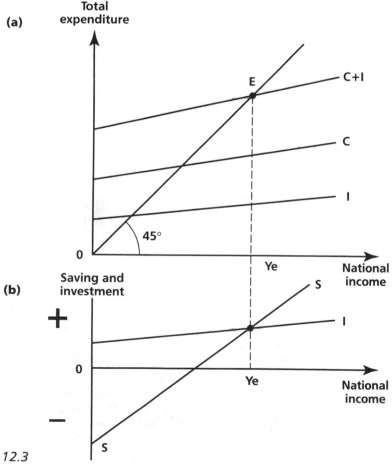

Figure 12.3

same point as the intersection of the saving and investment schedules. The equilibrium condition for national income is therefore the point where the C + I line intersects the 45° line; which is the same as saying that equilibrium is where income equals planned expenditure (E), i.e.

Y = E

at which point, as we can see from 12.3(b)

S = I Planned

11 Equilibrium and the circular flow

The equilibrium condition for national income S = I can be easily illustrated by the use of circular flow diagrams, as in Figure 12.4. In period 1 firms are paying out factor incomes (national income) of £100m to households. The chain of re-spending is not complete however because only £80m goes directly back to firms in the form of consumption because there are **leakages** from the circular flow in the form of savings which amount to £20m. This would not matter if the **injections** in the form of investment into the circular flow were also £20m.

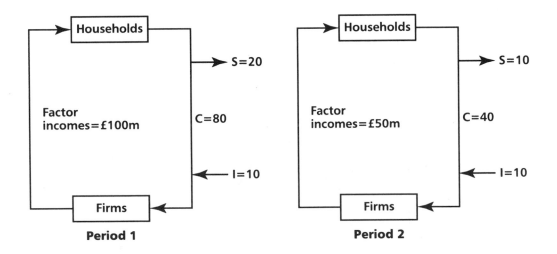

Figure 12.4

However, firms are only planning to invest £10m, therefore total receipts by firms are reduced and they will be unable to pay out the same amount in factor payments in period 2. In period 2 factor payments to households fall to £90m, i.e. **national income falls**. Incomes continue to fall until households are no longer planning to save more than firms are attempting to invest and when savings and investment are again equal at £10m equilibrium is established with national income = £50m. Had planned investment exceeded savings national income and therefore savings, would have risen until savings had risen sufficiently to match investment, again establishing equilibrium where S = I. (Assuming the MPC remains constant at 0.8).

12 Keynes and equilibrium

According to Keynes therefore it was **fluctuations in national income and therefore employment which brought about equilibrium between income and expenditure, and this equilibrium could be at any level of employment.**

13 National income and equilibrium

The equilibrium condition can also be explained in terms of national income analysis. From Chapter 1 we know that in equilibrium income (Y) is equal to expenditure (E).

therefore Y = E in equilibrium

As all income is either consumed (C) or saved (S), then

(1) Y = C + S

and as expenditure in our closed economy is either consumption or investment (I), then

(2) Y = C + I

As C can be eliminated from both equations 1 and 2, as it is common to both sides, we are left with the equilibrium condition

S = I

14 The three sector economy

We can now drop our assumption of no government activity and introduce the third element of total demand **government expenditure (G)**. When government expenditure is added to the private expenditures of consumption and investment we can derive what is referred to as **aggregate monetary demand (AMD)**, alternatively referred to as **effective demand.**

AMD = C + I + G

Figure 12.5 illustrates the separate C, I and G schedules, which together constitute the aggregate monetary demand curve of C + I + G, giving the equilibrium of income and expenditure at E (income Ye).

As we have discussed earlier however there is in the Keynesian model no reason why the equilibrium point E should coincide with the full employment level of income. In Figure 12.6 equilibrium E produces level of income Ye but the level of income consistent with full employment is Y', and equilibrium point E', unemployment is therefore present. The deficiency of AMD at the full employment level is E'–G, known as the **deflationary gap**. The problem is therefore how to shift the equilibrium level of income from E to E', the full employment level.

15 Changing equilibrium

Shifting equilibrium output from E to E' could be achieved by an increase in investment, but this would be unlikely to occur autonomously (independently), as firms facing a depressed level of sales would have little incentive to invest. What Keynes argued was

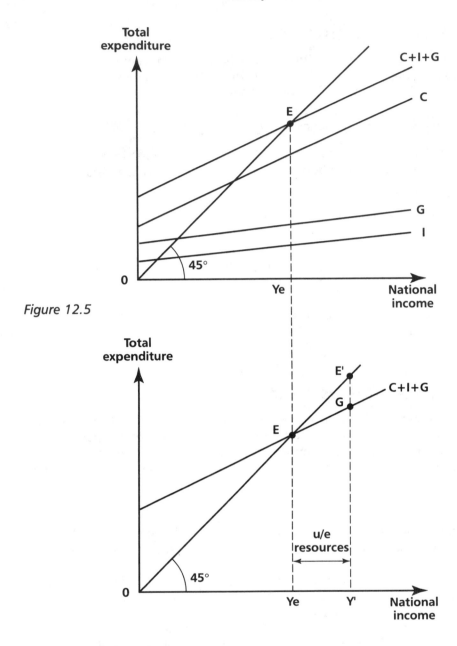

Figure 12.5

Figure 12.6

that governments should intervene in the economy and raise the level of their own expenditures, on for example public works projects, and boost the level of AMD to the full employment level. The increase in G would therefore represent an **injection** into the circular flow of income.

16 The multiplier

One essential point of the analysis is that the increase in G will not have to be as large as the required increase in AMD because of the **multiplier** process of re-spending. The simplest way to explain this re-spending process is to imagine an area of the country which has suffered high levels of unemployment and recession over a sustained period. The government then decides to build a major highway between two towns in the region and spend many millions of pounds on the project. The contract is placed with a construction company; however, before they can proceed they have to place orders for new construction equipment and materials, the suppliers of this equipment and materials have to employ additional labour to produce it, this labour is now in receipt of wages and proceeds to spend them, local businesses find they are selling more and place orders for additional supplies, the suppliers of which take on fresh labour and so on. In addition the construction firm will take on new direct labour for construction purposes, these workers will now make increased expenditures with local traders. A cycle of re-spending is started and each pound spent by the government will have an effect on final demand which is some multiple greater than itself. This is referred to as the **multiplier process**.

How large this multiplier process is depends upon how much is re-spent at each round, which is a function of the MPC and MPS of the income recipients. If they spend a high proportion of their incomes the multiplier will be larger than if a large proportion is saved at each round. The higher the MPC therefore the greater is the multiplier. This can be illustrated in Table 12.2 where the original government expenditure is £50, with an MPC of 0.7 and MPS of 0.3.

TABLE 12.2			
Spending round	Income (£)	Consumed (£)	Saved (£)
1st	50	35	15
2nd	35	24.50	10.50
3rd	24.50	17.50	7
4th	17.50	12.00	5.50
5th	12.00	8.40	3.60
6th	8.40	5.88	2.52
7th	5.88	4.10	1.78
8th	4.10	2.88	1.22
9th	2.88	2.00	.88
10th	2.00	1.40	.60
11th	1.40	.98	.42

The process continues until the amount of re-spending reduces to an infinitely small amount, and the total amount of income generated, or the multiplier effect, will be £166.66. This consists of the original £50 of government expenditure, referred to as autonomous expenditure; plus the re-spending generated at each successive round, referred to as **induced expenditure**.

17 The multiplier coefficient

The multiplier refers to the amount by which final income will be raised by any increase in government spending (or investment). The multiplier coefficient (usually represented by k) can be calculated by the formula

$$k = \frac{1}{1 - MPC}$$

or the reciprocal of the MPS. (The mathematically inclined will identify Table 12.2 as a geometric progression, the sum of which is the formula.)

In order to illustrate, let us assume that national income is £2000m and the government raises its expenditure by £50m, the effect on income is calculated as follows:

$$
\begin{aligned}
\text{National income} &= \text{£2000m} \\
\Delta G &= \text{£50m} \\
MPC &= 0.7
\end{aligned}
$$

$$\text{therefore } k = \frac{1}{1 - 0.7} = 3.33$$

$$50 \times 3.33 = 166.67$$

New national income = **£2166.67m**

(Note it is only the injection of £50m which is subject to the multiplier.)

18 The multiplier illustrated

The multiplier is illustrated in Figure 12.7. The economy is originally in equilibrium at E with income Y'. The full employment level of income is Yf, unemployment is Y'–Yf. An increase in G (ΔG) raises the AMD curve from E to the full employment equilibrium E' (income Yf). It should be noted that the increase in G is only about one third of the increase in Y, due to the effect of the multiplier. The effect of the multiplier can be estimated as

$$\frac{\Delta Y}{\Delta G}$$

19 Consumption and the multiplier

As the size of the multiplier is dependent upon the MPC, and we know that the MPC is the same as b in the formula for the consumption function C = a + b(Y), which is the slope of the curve, then graphically the steeper the slope of the AMD curve the greater the multiplier effect. In Figure 12.8 the increase in income from Y' to Yf was achieved by a much smaller increase in G when the AMD curve is steeper than when it has a shallow slope, this is because the steeper slope has a higher MPC (b) than the shallow slope, and the multiplier is correspondingly greater.

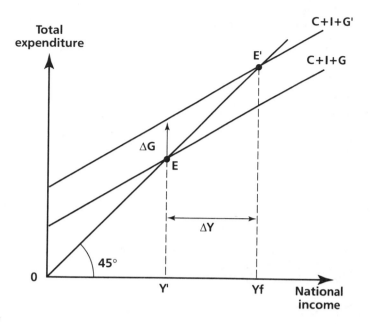

Figure 12.7

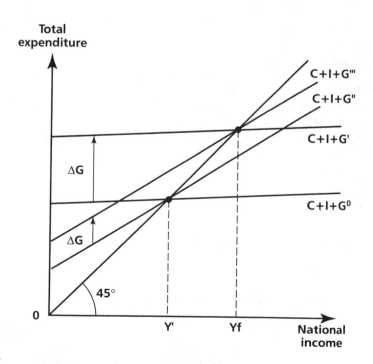

Figure 12.8

20 An open economy

We can now **drop our assumption of a closed economy** and allow for the effects of **imports** and **exports** in the form of the balance of payments surplus or deficit.

So far the only **injections** into the circular flow have been **investment (I)** and **government expenditure (G)**. We can now add a third, **exports (X)**, as selling goods abroad is an injection of purchasing power into the domestic economy.

The only **withdrawal** from the circular flow so far has been **saving (S)**. However, as we have introduced government expenditure we must also allow for the effects of **taxation (T)**; and as we now have an 'open' economy, for the effects of **imports (M)** which reduce purchasing power in the domestic economy.

Total injections	= Investment	+	Government expenditure	+ Exports
ie J	= I	+	G	+ X
Total Withdrawals =	Saving	+	Taxation	+ Imports
i.e. W	= S	+	T	+ M

21 Equilibrium

The **equilibrium condition** for national income now becomes

injections = withdrawals or

$$J = W$$

which is identical to our previous closed economy condition of S = I except that savings and investment are no longer the only injections and withdrawals from the circular flow.

22 MPM and MPT

In addition to the marginal propensities to consume and save we now have to accommodate the fact that some of any increment to income will be taken in **taxation** and some will be spent on **imports**, we therefore need to include in our analysis:

The marginal propensity to import (MPM) which is the amount of each increment to income which is spent on imports.

The marginal propensity to tax (MPT) which is the amount of each increment to income which is taken in tax (the tax rate).

Note that the **MPC + MPS + MPM + MPT = 1**.

23 The circular flow revisited

We can illustrate the principle again by the use of simple circular flow diagrams. (See Figure 12.9)

Diagram A represents an economy in equilibrium as the factor payments to households are received back by firms therefore **withdrawals are equal to injections**, i.e. J = W at £40m. It should also be noted that there is a balance of payments equilibrium (X = M) and the government has a balanced budget (G = T). Unemployment is however unacceptably high and it is estimated that the full employment income is £120m. In order to achieve this increase in income the government increases its expenditure by £8m which after the multiplier effect raises national income by £20m, a multiplier of 2.5. The government has achieved its full employment objective but note that this is only at the cost of 'trading-off' other equally desirable objectives.

A deficit has emerged on the balance of payments (i.e. imports = 12, exports = 10).

The government now has a deficit on its budget (taxation = 24, government expenditure = 28). This implies an increase in the **public sector borrowing requirement** which may have an inflationary impact on the price level.

There may be a fall in the exchange rate as a result of the balance of payments deficit which may add further inflationary pressure.

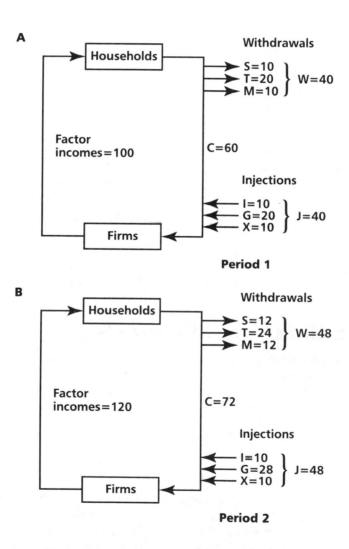

Figure 12.9

24 The new numerical multiplier

The multiplier (k) is now calculated by the following:

$$k = \frac{1}{1 - MPC}$$

$$or \quad \frac{1}{MPT + MPM + MPS}$$

e.g. MPC = 0.6
     MPM = 0.1
     MPS = 0.1
     MPT = 0.2

$$therefore \ k \ = \ \frac{1}{1 - 0.6} \ = \ \frac{1}{0.4} \ = 2.5$$

$$or \ k \ = \ \frac{1}{0.2 + 0.1 + 0.1} \ = \ \frac{1}{0.4} \ = 2.5$$

25 AMD

It is now possible to allow for an increase in AMD by an increase in either, or all, of the injections G, I or X. We will continue to assume however that the easiest of these variables for the government to manipulate is its own spending. Aggregate demand now however includes the effect of the **balance of payments deficit or surplus (X–M)**, hence our AMD schedule now becomes:

AMD = C + I + G + (X - M)

For brevity we will now identify the C + I + G + (X - M) line as AMD.

26 Injections and withdrawals

Previously we also utilised saving and investment functions, as these were the only withdrawals and injections, we can however follow the same analysis utilising an **injections function (J)** which represents I + G + X and a **withdrawals function (W)** representing S + T + M. It is not unreasonable to assume that all these functions rise with income and, as we have already established equilibrium is where J = W.

27 Equilibrium illustrated

We can illustrate the shift to a new equilibrium by utilising 45° line analysis as before or by using injections and withdrawals functions. In Figure 12.10 the economy is equilibrium at E with income Y below the full employment level Yf. In order to achieve full employment the government increases its expenditure, but it could be any of the injections G, I or X, i.e. ΔJ. This has the desired multiplier effect and shifts the AMD line to E',the size of the multiplier effect being

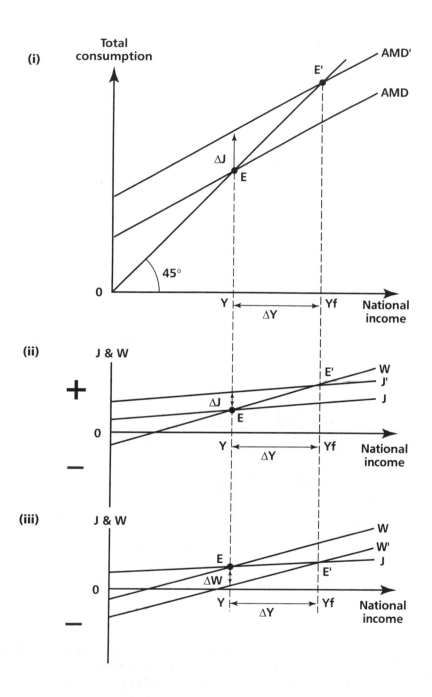

Figure 12.10

$$\frac{\Delta Y}{\Delta J}$$

and new equilibrium E' is at the full employment level of income Yf. In 12.10 (ii) this is represented as a shift in the injections function (J).

Original equilibrium is at E where J = W, the increased injections (ΔJ) shift J to J' and income rises until a new equilibrium is established where J = W again at E', and income Yf. The horizontal shift in Y being greater than the increase in G (i.e.ΔJ) due to the multiplier effect, which can again be estimated as

$$\frac{\Delta Y}{\Delta J}$$

Exactly the same result could have been achieved by reducing withdrawals and in Figure 12.10 (iii) this is represented by a shift of the withdrawals function (W) down from W to W' whilst injections remain constant. Income rises as a consequence and continues to do so until J = W again at E' and income has risen from Y to Yf. The size of the multiplier effect being

$$\frac{\Delta Y}{\Delta W}$$

With the inclusion of the additional variables it is evident that there are other policy instruments available to the government in addition to its own expenditure which can be used to boost the level of demand, for example reductions in direct or indirect taxes, encouragement to private investment or assisting exports. It is more likely in fact to be a 'policy mix' rather than total reliance on a single policy instrument.

28 Fiscal and monetary policy

Policy measures are generally referred to as being either **fiscal** or **monetary.**

- **Fiscal policy** generally refers to changes in **government expenditure** and **taxation**.
- **Monetary policy** generally refers to the control of the money supply (open market operations etc.), control of the banking system, and interest rate policy.
- **Direct controls** operate directly upon the policy objective, e.g. incomes policy.
- In reality the distinction between fiscal and monetary policy is not quite so straight-forward, for example the PSBR is one of the most important influences on the money supply but arises as a **consequence** of the level of government expenditure (fiscal policy).

29 The 'downward' multiplier

In the analysis so far we have assumed that the multiplier is utilised to increase AMD during a period of deficient demand. The process could be reversed and in a period of excess demand the inflationary pressures reduced by selecting the appropriate policy mix of reduced government spending and increased taxation to produce a 'downward' multiplier effect. Experience indicates however that Keynesian policies have been less successful in dealing with inflation than unemployment.

30 The government budget

Prior to Keynes the annual budget was similar to a book-keeping exercise whereby the sources of tax revenue and how the government intended to spend it was outlined, and there was generally a belief that as far as possible the budget should balance. The implication of Keynes' analysis was that the government should deliberately aim for an unbalanced budget.

- In a situation of deficient demand and recession the government should spend more than it gathers in tax revenue and run a **budget deficit.**
- In a situation of excess demand and inflation a government may in theory attempt to gather more in taxation than it spends and run a **budget surplus**. During the post-war period budget deficits were the norm however a budget surplus was established in the UK between 1987 and 1989. As the budget surplus is available for debt repayment it is referred to as the **public sector debt repayment (PSDR)**.
- A further possibility is the **balanced budget**. For a balanced budget government revenue is equal to its expenditure. This may be politically attractive to governments, particularly so when it is still possible to have a multiplier effect. The multiplier effect with a balanced budget is referred to as the **balanced budget multiplier.** (This concept is developed further in Appendix 2).

31 The Keynesian approach

Keynes advocated that the increased government spending could be financed by the government borrowing from wealth holders. The additional income created would generate sufficient tax revenue to repay the borrowing, and those finding employment would now be taxpayers rather than receivers of benefits. The process would not be inflationary provided domestic output could grow sufficiently rapidly. The additional borrowing does however imply an increase in the PSBR.

Keynes' ideas were first tried in the USA with the 'New Deal' in 1933, where projects such as the Tennessee Valley Authority scheme were undertaken. Most countries however based the management of their economies on Keynesian principles in the period following 1945 until inflation became the overriding concern during the mid 1970s, and the emphasis changed towards the control of the money supply as being the most important policy instrument.

Self assessment questions

1 What is the consumption function?
2 What is the marginal propensity to consume and how it calculated?
3 State the equilibrium condition for a closed economy with no government sector.
4 State the components of aggregate monetary demand in an open economy with government activity.
5 State the equilibrium conditions for an open economy with taxation and government spending.
6 Given an MPC of 0.8 calculate the size of the multiplier.

7 Discuss the affects of an increase in government expenditure on the level of aggregate demand.

8 The businessperson should be aware of the multiplier effect because of its importance in their business operation. Explain why this is so.

Appendix 1

Where fiscal policy involves a change in direct taxation the analysis of the multiplier is slightly different to that for government expenditure. Using b = MPC for brevity the effect of a change in government expenditure was given above as

$$\Delta Y = \frac{1}{1-b}\Delta G$$

and the multiplier coefficient was therefore:

$$\frac{\Delta Y}{\Delta G} = \frac{1}{1-b}$$

An increase in taxation, however, will reduce the level of disposable income for any level of national income, shifting the AMD curve downwards as it reduces the level of consumption spending. The downward shift in consumption, however, will be less than the increase in taxation because some of the tax increase will be absorbed by reduced saving. Changes in government spending and investment therefore have a pound for pound effect on AMD, whilst changes in taxation have an effect which is a fraction of their magnitude. A change in taxation changes AMD by the fraction (-b) of the tax change only as (1–b) is absorbed in reduced savings. This fraction (-b) multiplied by the full expenditure multiplier [1/(1–b)] gives the multiplier for the effect on equilibrium income of a change in taxation, i.e.

$$\left(\frac{1}{1-b}\right)$$

Hence for the effect of a change in taxation we have

$$\Delta Y = \frac{1}{1-b}(-b)\Delta T$$

and the tax multiplier is therefore:

$$\frac{\Delta Y}{\Delta T} = \frac{-b}{1-b}$$

It is important to note therefore that impact of policy measure on the economy may vary because the multiplier effects may vary.

Appendix 2

The **balanced budget multiplier** arises because, as outlined in Appendix 1 above, the negative tax multiplier is always less in value than the government spending multiplier. In order to assess the combined effect of an increase in government expenditure financed from an equivalent increase in taxation the two multipliers are added together:

$$\frac{\Delta Y}{\Delta G} + \frac{\Delta Y}{\Delta T} = \frac{1}{1-b} + \frac{-b}{1-b} = \frac{1-b}{1-b} = 1$$

i.e. The **balanced budget multiplier = UNITY (1)**, hence a £1 increase in government expenditure financed from a £1 tax increase will increase national income by £1.

13

Demand management in practice

1 Policy objectives

The objectives of economic policy can be stated as:

- **full employment**
- **stable prices**
- **balance of payments equilibrium**
- **economic growth**

In achieving any one of these objectives governments may have to accept a deterioration or 'trade-off' in one or more equally desirable policy targets.

2 Keynesian policies

The use of Keynesian policies in the 1950s and 1960s prevented any return to the mass unemployment of the 1930s, the era was, however, characterised by what has been referred to as 'stop-go' policies as governments attempted to achieve their policy targets, but found them difficult to achieve simultaneously. Following Beveridge (1944) full employment was generally accepted to be about 3% unemployment. As unemployment rose above this figure measures would be taken to expand the economy by appropriate fiscal policy measures (government spending and taxation) in order to increase the level of economic activity and reduce unemployment. The increase in demand however also had the effect of increasing imports because not all of the additional demand was met from domestic output, and also of raising the price level which made UK exports less competitive, consequently a balance of payments deficit emerged. This put downward pressure on the exchange rate and under its commitment to maintain the exchange rate the government would be forced to intervene and use the foreign exchange reserves in support of sterling. The achievement of the full employment objective had been at the cost of price stability and the balance of payments. In order to stabilise the price level and eliminate the deficit on the balance of payments the government would then introduce deflationary policies in order to dampen down demand, the rate of price increase would stabilise and an improvement in the balance of payments would be achieved at the cost of higher unemployment, hence the reference to 'stop-go' policies. One of the arguments against the 'stop-go' cycle was that it created a climate of uncertainty and therefore interfered with investment plans and reduced long term growth prospects. The period also saw repeated attempts to introduce **incomes policies** which were intended to keep the rate of wage increase within the increase in productivity in order to allow the economy to be run closer to full employment whilst avoiding the inflationary effects. Unfortunately during the most stringent periods of incomes policy costs rose due to non wage factors, e.g. oil in 1973/74.

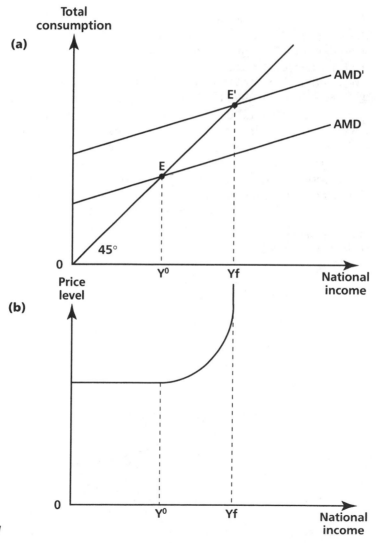

Figure 13.1

3 AMD and the price level

The Keynesian model outlined in the previous chapter ignored any effect the increase in AMD may have had on the price level. In Figure 13. 1(a) equilibrium is shifted from E to E', the full employment level, by an appropriate fiscal policy mix. In the lower diagram (b) however, it can be seen that prices are relatively stable until full resource utilisation is approached when they begin to rise progressively. At full employment output cannot be raised further and the rate of increase becomes almost vertical. Where there are unemployed resources therefore a reflation of the economy through fiscal policy would initially raise real output and employment with a modest rise in the price level, but as full employment is approached further increases in demand result only in a rise in the rate of inflation.

4 The Phillips curve

The 'trade-off' between inflation and unemployment was formalised in the **Phillips curve**. A.W. Phillips (1958), using data covering the period 1861–1957, identified a close correlation between the rate of change of money wages and employment. As wages are the most significant influence on prices the Phillips curve can also be expressed as the relationship between inflation (rate of change of prices) and unemployment, as illustrated in Figure 13.2. On the curve rates of inflation can be identified for each level of unemployment. Stable wages should be achieved at 5½% unemployment. The employment target of 3% would be associated with a modest level of inflation, and as employment is reduced below this there is ever accelerating inflation. Very high levels of unemployment such as x may even be associated with falling prices (y). Note that as the curve approaches full resources utilisation it becomes progressively steeper, hence at low levels of unemployment further reductions become more costly in terms of inflation. The Phillips curve was very accurate in predicting wage increases over the period 1958–1966,

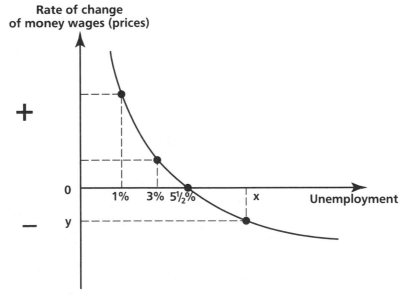

Figure 13.2 The Phillips curve

however the concept of the Phillips curve took a severe blow during the period 1974/75 when unemployment actually rose to 5½% but rather than price stability price increases of over 20% were being recorded. (This is discussed further in Chapter 17).

5 The monetarist view

Monetarists (see Chapter 16) suggest that the budget deficits resulting from demand management policies and the increase in the public sector borrowing requirement that this implies, results in an increase in the money supply and as a consequence leads to inflation.

The use of government spending described in the Keynesian model is also criticised on the grounds that the government expenditure would merely replace or '**crowd out**' an equivalent amount of private expenditure. Keynes suggested however that the multiplier effect would generate a sufficient increase in total expenditure to prevent this.

Crowding out may however happen as a result of the increase in interest rates which result from the budget deficit. In order to raise the necessary debt finance the government issues debt instruments (Treasury bills and gilts) which compete with the private demand for finance and raises the interest rate. The increase in the interest rate may reduce any private investment expenditures which are interest rate elastic (i.e. sensitive to interest rate changes). This implies that total expenditure may not increase by as much as the traditional multiplier suggests.

6 Slumpflation

The new phenomenon which arose in the mid 1970s of rising unemployment and simultaneously rising prices, referred to as **slumpflation** or **stagflation** suggested that the previously accepted relationships had broken down and were difficult to accommodate within orthodox demand management policies. In particular the Keynesian tradition of demand management and the relationships explicit with the orthodox Phillips curve came under attack. Some of the criticisms of the Keynesian model have been outlined above but these and the criticisms of the Phillips curve will be discussed in more detail in later chapters.

Self assessment questions

1 Outline the 'stop-go' cycle.
2 Discuss the relationship between increases in aggregate demand and the price level.
3 What are the implications for the relationship between prices and employment contained within the Phillips curve?
4 Why was the period of the mid 1970s referred to as an era of 'stagflation'?
5 How might government spending 'crowd-out' private spending?

14

The accelerator

1 A definition

The **accelerator** is a **capital stock adjustment process** which relates changes in the capital stock to the **rate of change of national income**.

2 Derived demand

The demand for capital is a **derived demand**, as capital is not demanded for its own sake, but for what it will produce, it therefore reflects changes in consumer demand which is itself dependent upon income. The accelerator principle suggests that any change in income (consumption) will be reflected in a magnified form in the output of the capital goods industries.

3 The accelerator principle

In order to illustrate this principle we will assume that in the production of brake cylinders for cars there is a fixed ratio between output and the number of lathes required (capital stock). If we assume that 10 lathes are required to produce 1000 cylinders and each lathe lasts for 10 years, as long as demand remains constant at 1000 cylinders each year the firm will just replace the one lathe which wears out each year. However if as a result of an increase in income demand rises to 1100 cylinders, an increase of 10%, the firm will now have to order 2 lathes, 1 replacement machine plus 1 to provide the additional capacity, therefore the demand for lathes, and therefore the output of the lathe industry, has risen by 100%. A 10% increase in consumption has resulted in a 100% increase in the output of the capital goods industry, i.e. an 'accelerated effect' If income continues to rise at 10% per annum then the output of both industries will continue to grow; however, if eventually consumption ceases to grow and the firms supplying brakes and other components to the car industry find they have sufficient capital to meet current demand, investment demand will return to replacement demand and in the example the demand for lathes would return to 1 each year, a 50% fall in the output of the lathe industry, again an accelerated effect of the change in consumption but this time operating in reverse. A reduction in investment demand can therefore occur as a result merely of a failure of consumption to increase. If consumption actually declines then the firm may find it has excess capacity and may not even replace its worn out machines. This 'naïve' accelerator provides one explanation for the pronounced cyclical upturns and downturns in the output of the capital goods industries.

4 A numerical example

The accelerator principle is illustrated here using the same example but with data to make the relationship clearer.

TABLE 14.1						
	Year	Brake cylinders	Lathes	Gross investment (replacement plus net investment)	Net investment	
Phase 1	Year 1	1000	10	1	0	
	Year 2	1000	10	1	0	
	Year 3	1000	10	1	0	
Phase 2	Year 4	1100	11	2	1	100% increase in lathe production
	Year 5	1200	12	2	1	
Phase 3	Year 6	1300	13	2	1	100% decline in lathe production
	Year 7	1300	13	1	0	
Phase 4	Year 8	1200	12	0	0	Lathe production fallen to zero – disinvestment

Gross investment includes replacement investment plus net investment. Only net investment increases the capital stock and it is possible to have gross investment but no net investment. The demand for brake cylinders depends upon consumption (or income). The demand for the latter is derived from the demand for brake cylinders. In Phase 1, assuming the firm replaces one lathe each year, then gross investment is one lathe per year which consists only of replacement investment to replace the one lathe worn out. In year 4, income rises and the consumption of brake cylinders rises to 1100 – requiring a capital stock of 11 lathes. Gross investment now consists of one replacement plus one new machine, i.e. a 100% increase in the output of the capital goods industry. There is no problem as long as incomes continue to rise throughout phase 2; however in phase 3 income ceases to rise so investment falls back to replacement investment as the existing capital stock is sufficient. In phase 4, year 8, income falls slightly and there is dis-investment with the worn out machine not being replaced. Note that merely a failure of income to rise at the previous rate was sufficient to cause a 50% downswing in the fortunes of the capital goods industry. These violent upturns and downturns in the fortunes of the capital goods industry are referred to as the accelerator.

5 The accelerator relationship

The 'naïve' or simple accelerator can be expressed as follows. If we assume a direct relationship between income (GDP) and the stock of capital required to produce it, then

$$K = \alpha Y$$

where

K = the stock of capital
Y = income (GDP)
α = the coefficient (ratio) which relates the level of capital stock to the level of output.

Changes in the stock of capital are the same thing as investment therefore $\Delta K = I$, and

$$I = \alpha \Delta Y \quad \text{(or alternatively } I = \alpha \Delta C)$$

6 Dampening factors

In reality the accelerator effect may not be as extreme as suggested in the example and the effect may be dampened by a number of factors.

- Firms will not automatically increase investment at the first sign of an increase in sales, they may prefer to wait until they become convinced that the increase in sales is permanent. They may rationalise that some loss in sales in the short-run is less expensive than a bad investment decision.
- There may be some excess capacity in the industry which can be utilised before new investment becomes necessary. It may even be possible to use existing capacity more intensively, for example by working extra shifts. Although this may raise costs it may still be cheaper than re-investing to meet a temporary increase in demand.
- The capital goods industries may not be able to respond quickly to an increase in demand and it may take a considerable time for them to adjust their own capacity.

The accelerator may therefore be subject to considerable time lags. In order to incorporate these lags several other accelerator models have been developed, these lagged accelerator models can be found in most more advanced texts.

7 The accelerator and the trade cycle

The accelerator principle may explain the upper and lower turning points of the trade cycle. If as a result of an increase in income there is an increase in investment and a growth in the output of the capital goods industries the additional investment will generate a multiplier effect on incomes and a further rise in consumption and further new investment. The accelerator and multiplier interact with each other in an upward spiral. Eventually however the full employment ceiling will be reached and output cannot increase, or at least slows down. As the rate of growth of incomes slows down, or ceases, the accelerator effect operates in the opposite direction and the stabilising of consumption has a magnified downward effect on the capital goods industries. The reduction in investment has a downwards multiplier effect on consumption and multiplier and accelerator interact in a downward spiral into recession. If the economy has been in a prolonged recession with low levels of consumer demand, firms will eventually have to make a choice between reinvesting to replace worn out plant or going out of business. As plant becomes worn out or obsolete and firms are forced to reinvest they set the upward spiral in motion again. This of course is a highly simplified outline of the process, but does provide one explanation of the upper and lower turning points of the trade cycle.

Self assessment questions

1 What is the 'driving force' behind the accelerator principle?
2 Outline the relationship between changes in consumption and the output of the capital goods industries.
3 What factors may dampen the accelerator effect?
4 Examine how the interaction of the multiplier and the accelerator may cause trade cycles or fluctuations in the national income.

15

Interest rate determination and investment

In this chapter we will briefly outline the Keynesian view of interest and money.

1 Discount rate and net present value

We will consider first the relationship between interest rates and the firm's investment plans. A firm considering any investment proposal will attempt to estimate the addition to profits which will be forthcoming from the investment project. These additions to profit will not however be made in a single time period but will be received over several years. In order to estimate the net benefit of the investment it is necessary therefore to estimate the **net present value** of the future returns by means of a **discount** factor. To explain this more simply, imagine the alternatives of £100 received today or £100 received in 1 year's time with a current interest rate of 10%. If the £100 received today had been invested for 1 year it would have been worth £110, alternatively we would only need to invest £91 today for it to be worth £100 in 1 year's time. Hence £100 in 1 year's, time is worth only £91 today. In other words future income receipts are worth less than present income receipts. For this reason estimates of future income receipts from an investment project have to be discounted by an appropriate **discount rate** in order to find the **present value**, the process being similar to compound interest in reverse. The discount rate represents the **opportunity cost of capital,** which is in fact the **rate of interest**; as the outlay involved in the project could have been invested and have earned interest with zero risk. The present value of the annual inflows is summed and compared with the cost of buying the machine (C), if the present value is greater than the cost the net present value will be positive and the project goes ahead, and vice versa.

2 Discounted cash flow

This process, referred to as **discounted cash flow**, can be represented as:

$$NPV = \frac{Y_1}{(1 + r)} + \frac{Y_2}{(1 + r)^2} + \frac{Y_3}{(1 + r)^3} + \dots \frac{Y_n}{(1 + r)^n}$$

The income or yield from the investment (Y) is discounted each year by the appropriate discount rate (r) over the relevant number of years (n). The discount rate is simply the percentage rate expressed as a decimal, i.e. if the percentage rate is 6% then r = 0.06, so in the first year (I + r) = 1.06, in year 2 the discount factor is $(1.06)^2$ and so on. Normally however it is unnecessary to calculate this as tables are available, or more commonly today the calculation is carried out by computer, utilising one of the investment appraisal packages available. Discounted cash flow is normally represented by the following formula:

$$NPV = \sum_{i=1}^{n} \frac{Y}{(1+r)^n}$$

where   NPV   =   Net present value
              Y   =   Income or yield from the investment
              Σ =   sum of
              n   =   number of years the project will last
              r   =   discount rate

The discount factor can be found from a standard NPV table, an extract from which is given below in table 15.1

TABLE 15.1

Present   Value of £1

Year	1%	2%	3%	4%	5%	6%
1	0.990	0.980	0.971	0.961	0.952	0.943
2	0.980	0.961	0.943	0.925	0.907	0.890
3	0.971	0.942	0.915	0.889	0.864	0.840
4	0.961	0.924	0.889	0.855	0.823	0.792
5	0.951	0.906	0.863	0.822	0.784	0.747

Whenever the result of the calculation produces a negative outcome a project should not go ahead as the investment is not producing a return greater than the opportunity cost of the capital, which would earn more in an alternative financial investment such as the bank. Alternatively if the choice is between two projects then the one which yields the greatest NPV should be chosen. For example, supposing a firm can invest £20,000 in either of two alternative investments or could leave the capital in the bank earning 6% per annum. The income (or yield) from the sale of the output from the two projects is estimated as follows.

YEAR END AMOUNT £s					
	Year 1	Year 2	Year 3	Year 4	Year 5
Project A	- 20,000	4,000	5,000	6,000	8,000
Project B	- 20,000	8,000	6,000	5,000	4,000

(Note that the - 20,000 in Year 1 indicates the capital outlay.)
The capital inflows and outflows are then multiplied by the appropriate discount factor to find the NPV of both projects.

PROJECT A					
	Year 1	Year 2	Year 3	Year 4	Year 5
Outflow (£s)	- 20,000				
Inflow (£s)		4,000	5,000	6,000	8,000
Discount factor (6%)	0.943	0.890	0.840	0.792	0.747
NPV	-18,860	3,560	4,200	4,752	5,976
Cumulative NPV	-18,860	-15,300	-11,100	-6,348	-372
NET PRESENT VALUE = -£372					

The project should be rejected as it yields a negative NPV.

PROJECT B					
	Year 1	Year 2	Year 3	Year 4	Year 5
Outflow (£s)	- 20,000				
Inflow (£s)		8,000	6,000	5,000	4,000
Discount factor (6%)	0.943	0.890	0.840	0.792	0.747
NPV	-18,860	7,120	5,040	3,960	2,988
Cumulative NPV	-18,860	-11,740	-6,700	-2,740	248
NET PRESENT VALUE = £248					

This project should be accepted as it yields a positive NPV i.e Project B offers a greater return than Project A. Note that this is despite the fact that the total income over the 5 years is identical (£23,000) - it is the timing of the income which is crucial.

3 Internal rate of return

An alternative approach based on exactly the same principles as those outlined above is referred to as the **internal rate of return (IRR)**. This can be summarised as

$$PV = \sum_{i=1}^{n} \frac{Y}{(1+x)^n}$$

where   x = IRR

The firm estimates the value of x (the internal rate of return) which produces a present value equal to the cost of the machine, i.e. finds that x which produces PV = C. The firm will rationally invest in the machine whenever the **internal rate of return is greater than the rate of interest,** i.e. x is greater than r.

4 The marginal efficiency of capital

The internal rate of return is also referred to as the **marginal efficiency of capital (MEC)**. It will pay a firm to invest and increase its stock of capital up to the point where the MEC is equal to the interest rate.

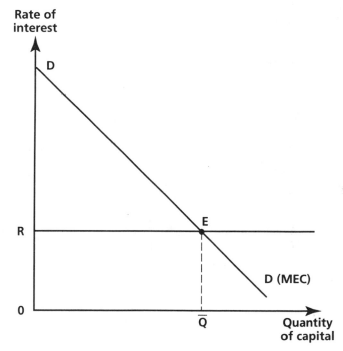

Figure 15.1

If however the stock of capital is increased, relative to other factors, then like the other factors of production it will be subject to **diminishing marginal productivity**. As a consequence the MEC declines as the capital stock is increased, and if represented diagramatically it slopes downwards to the right and constitutes the firm's **demand curve for capital.** It slopes downwards because the most profitable investments will be undertaken first and further investments will be less profitable as marginal productivity declines, and will therefore only be undertaken at lower rates of interest. The profit maximising firm will be in equilibrium regarding its capital stock when the **marginal efficiency of capital is equal to the rate of interest,** i.e.

$$MEC = R$$

In Figure 15.1 the firm is in equilibrium at E with capital stock $\bar{Q}$ when the rate of interest is R.

The firm would only increase its stock of capital if either the rate of interest fell, or the MEC of capital increased; through for example the introduction of new technology.

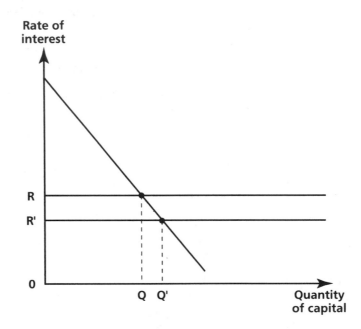

Figure 15.2

In Figure 15.2 a fall in the rate of interest from R to R' raises the firm's optimal stock of capital from Q to Q'. An increase in the rate of interest would have the reverse effect.

In Figure 15.3 the MEC of capital has increased as a result of the introduction of new technology with greater productivity this has shifted the MEC curve outwards from MEC to MEC' raising the firm's optimal capital stock from Q to Q' at R rate of interest.

In both cases if the firm changes its capital stock to the new optimal level then the change in the capital stock, i.e. Q to Q' represents **net investment.**

5 The demand for money

We have so far taken the rate of interest as given, however in order to consider how the rate of interest is determined it is necessary to consider the demand for money. The demand for money does not refer to the demand for money for spending on goods, but the demand for the actual stock of money to hold as money balances. It will be recalled from Chapter 12 that according to 'classical theory' money was only held for purposes of

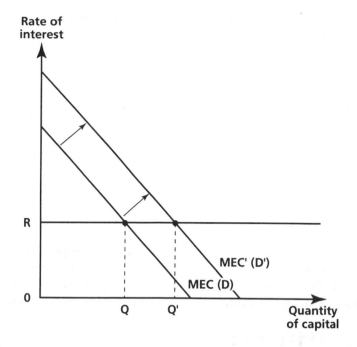

Figure 15.3

making transactions and bridging the time period between income receipts, however Keynes added the possibility of the demand for money as an asset, i.e. speculative balances. Three 'motives' for demanding money balances are identified as:

- **Transactions demand** – as in classical theory transactions balances were needed to bridge the gap between receipts and expenditure. The size of such balances is dependent upon:
  - **The length of time** between receipts and expenditure.
  - The **size** of receipts and expenditure. Transactions balances would vary with income and **not** rates of interest.
- **Precautionary demand** – money will be held for the purpose of meeting unforeseen emergencies. This motive was not included in classical theory where perfect certainty was assumed. Keynes grouped transactions and precautionary balances together into a single sum which varied directly with the **level of income**.
- **Speculative demand** – the speculative motive was Keynes' innovation. In order to understand this motive it is necessary to ask, why should people hold money balances over and above those described above when money is an asset which yields no return at all? The answer to this is that if other financial assets, in particular bonds, are likely to fall in price then losses on bonds can be avoided by holding money instead. The motive for holding speculative money balances is therefore to avoid losses in a declining securities market. In order to understand this more clearly it is necessary to consider the relationship between bond prices and the rate of interest. In this context Keynes was referring to undated government securities (referred to as 'gilts' or 'consols'). These bonds pay a fixed annual sum and are bought and sold on the securities market, their price therefore varies with demand and supply. For example, if an undated security has a nominal value of £200 and pays £10 per annum, the nominal interest

(or coupon) is 5%. However, the actual yield or earnings yield, expressed as a rate of interest, will vary inversely with the market price of the security.

Normal price	£10 annual payment expressed as % of nominal price	Market price	(Earnings yield) = Rate of interest
£ 200	5%	£400	2½%
£ 200	5%	£200	5%
£ 200	5%	£100	10%

For example, it can be seen that as the market price rises to £400 the fixed annual payment of £10 represents the equivalent of an earnings yield of 2½% rate of interest and when the price falls to £100 the rate of interest rises to 10%. The market price and rate of interest, i.e. earnings yield, on fixed interest bonds is therefore **inversely related**.

6 Liquidity preference

Speculative money balances vary therefore with the anticipated gains or losses on the securities market, and the extent to which individuals prefer holdings of money to other financial assets is referred to as **liquidity preference**. Bearing in mind the relationship between security prices and interest rates above we can make the following assumptions.

- When security prices are high (and interest rates are low) speculators will expect bond prices to fall and therefore a capital loss to be made. They will therefore attempt to avoid such losses by holding speculative money balances. Low interest rates therefore imply a high liquidity preference. Note also that the opportunity cost of holding money is lower.
- When bond prices are low (and interest rates therefore are high) speculators will anticipate a rise in bond prices and therefore a capital gain. They will attempt to take advantage of the capital gain on bonds by holding bonds rather than money balances. High interest rates therefore imply a low liquidity preference. Note also that the opportunity cost of holding money is higher.

7 Expectations

It is important to note the importance of speculators' expectations about the future course of interest rates. Each individual is assumed to hold their expectations with complete certainty, although there may be disagreement between individuals about the future course of interest rates.

8 The liquidity preference curve

If each individual's liquidity preference is added together a **liquidity preference curve** can be drawn, which represents the **demand for money**. The liquidity preference curve relates the total demand for money to the rate of interest. Although each individual may have different expectations of future events, by adding them all together we obtain the smooth liquidity preference curve in Figure 15.4.

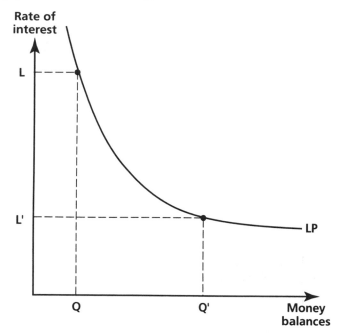

Figure 15.4

In Figure 15.4 when the interest rate is L bond prices will be low and a rise in bond prices, and therefore capital gains, will be anticipated and speculative balances will be zero, only transactions and precautionary balances being held, i.e. Q. When the rate of interest is low at L′ and bond prices are high capital losses are anticipated and larger speculative money balances are held, i.e. Q′ in order to avoid capital losses on bonds. The horizontal portion of the liquidity preference curve is referred to as the **liquidity trap**. In this portion of the curve the demand for money is infinitely elastic with respect to the interest rate. Reductions in the interest rate, in this portion only, increases people's desire to hold cash balances. The implication here is that any attempt to achieve internal expansion through increased investment brought about by lowering the interest rate would fail, because any increase in the money supply created in order to reduce the rate of interest would be held in the form of cash balances, making it impossible to use interest rates (monetary policy) to expand the economy.

9 Money supply

The **supply of money** at any point of time is fixed by the monetary authorities and is therefore independent of the rate of interest. In Figure 15.5 the money supply is therefore the vertical line MS. The rate of interest is determined where the demand for money (LP) intersects the supply (MS), at interest rate R.

Changes in the interest rate could occur as a result of:

- A shift in the liquidity preference curve as a result of anticipated changes in bond prices.
- A shift in the money supply curve by the authorities changing the supply of money. Note that an increase in the horizontal portion, the liquidity trap, would leave interest rates unchanged and would be held entirely in the form of additional money balances making monetary policy weak and ineffectual.

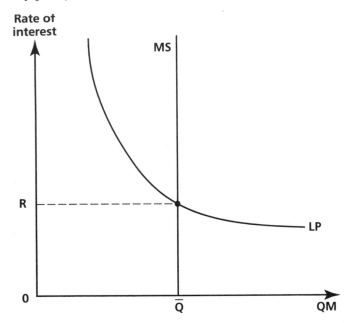

Figure 15.5

10 Changes in money supply

According to conventional liquidity preference theory an increase in the money supply in the 'normal' range of the liquidity preference curve will result in a reduction in the rate of interest which should increase the firm's optimal stock of capital and therefore result in an increase in investment. In Figure 15.6 the authorities increase the money supply from Ms to Ms' and as a consequence the rate of interest falls from R to R'; the effect of this on investment is shown in Figure 15.7, where the fall in the interest rate from R to R'increases the firm's optimal stock of capital from Q to Q'. This increase in investment would not occur if the demand for money was perfectly elastic as in the 'liquidity trap' situation (see section 8 above).

Further as Keynes suggested, firms' investment plans depend also upon their view of the future. If their expectations of future sales were pessimistic a lower rate of interest may not be sufficient inducement to undertake investment and national income would remain unchanged. It was for precisely this reason that Keynes advocated the use of government expenditure. The way in which the increase in the money supply is financed may also be important, because, as is explained in the following chapter, if the increase in the money supply is a result of an increase in the public sector borrowing requirement, a consequence of this may be a rise in the price level and a return to a higher level of interest rates with at best only a temporary effect on the level of investment and output. Conventional liquidity preference may also fail to operate during a period of inflation because bonds are only one example of a portfolio of assets which may be held as an alternative to money, and during a period of inflation other assets such as houses and land may offer a better hedge against inflation than bonds which will have low prices, because a high yield will be required in order to compensate for inflation.

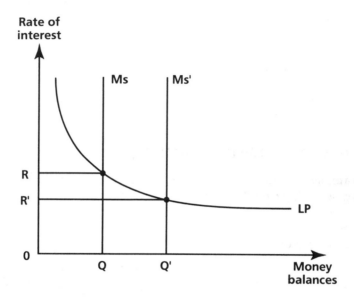

Figure 15.6

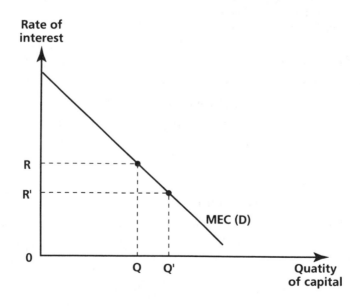

Figure 15.7

11 Sales expectations

Keynes, it should be noted, suggested that the investment decisions by firms were only marginally influenced by interest rates, the major factor being **sales expectations**. Firms would invest if they expected the future level of demand and therefore profits to be high.

12 Different views

In classical theory the rate of interest brings equality between savings and investment; however in Keynesian theory savings and investment are brought into balance through changes in income operating through the multiplier process.

Keynesian theory emphasises the effect of interest rates on real activity through the effects on investment, and through the multiplier effect, on income.

Monetarists (see Chapter 16) stress the effects of interest rates on the money supply and inflation.

13 The interest rate spectrum

The interest rate here refers to the basic rate of interest on government undated bonds. There is of course a whole spectrum of other interest rates, e.g.

- Building societies
- Hire purchase
- Bank deposit accounts
- Private tenders etc.

Each will have a different rate of interest which is determined by factors such as:

- The duration of the loan.
- The degree of risk, in particular the credit-worthiness of the borrower.
- The amount of collateral available.
- The purpose and nature of the loan.

Self assessment questions

1 What is meant by the marginal efficiency of capital?

2 How does the firm determine its optimal stock of capital?

3 Discuss why the speculative demand for money varies with the rate of interest.

4 What is meant by liquidity preference?

5 How does liquidity preference and the money supply determine the rate of interest?

6 What is meant by the net present value of an investment?

7 How is the internal rate of return calculated?

8 What is the affect of an increase in the money supply on the, firm's demand for capital?

16

Monetarism and inflation

1 A definition

The expression 'monetarist' is a general term used to describe those economists who believe that the money supply is the most important factor in determining the level of expenditure and prices.

2 Monetarist origins

The monetarist concepts have their origins in classical economics, however their revival in modified form owes much to Professor Milton Friedman. Friedman and Schwartz (A.J.) analysed data in the USA between 1867 and 1960 and demonstrated a close correlation (relationship) between changes in the money supply and the rate of change of money GDP, and therefore prices, after a time lag of about 18 months. Friedman suggested therefore that there was a strong causal relationship between the supply of money and inflation.

3 Friedman's views

Friedman states that 'inflation is always and everywhere a monetary phenomenon', meaning that inflation is always due to an excessive growth in the money supply. Several historical examples are quoted such as the influx of gold from S. America into Europe in the 16th Century, the gold finds in California in 1849, and those in Australia and S. Africa in the late 19th and early 20th centuries: all of which were followed by a rapid rise in prices. Friedman suggests that those examples have their modern counterparts in the budget deficits of the second half of the 20th century.

4 Causes of inflation

As inflation is caused only by increasing the money supply the implication is that as only governments can print money, then only governments cause inflation. Only governments therefore can cure inflation – by keeping a tight control over the supply of money. Governments can always obtain the resources they require by increasing the supply of money which raises the price level. The increase in the price level reduces real incomes which enables the government to acquire a greater share of the available resources. This is identical to the effect of taxation, hence Friedman refers to expansion of the money supply as 'taxation without representation'.

The increase in the money supply arises from the budget deficits which governments maintain in order to pursue fiscal policies which will maintain aggregate demand at levels consistent with full employment. Governments are pressed to maintain high levels of expenditure but they are unwilling to raise taxation in order to pay for it and so resort to deficit financing. (See Chapter 12). As suggested above, this is a hidden form of taxation due to the effect on the price level and therefore real incomes.

5 The money supply

At this stage it is worth reiterating exactly what we mean by the money supply. The most important definition in this context is the broader definition M4 which it will be recalled from Chapter 10 is defined as:

Notes and coins in circulation + current and deposit accounts held by all UK residents in sterling in banks and building societies.

The money supply therefore includes not only notes and coin but also the banks' ability to create credit. An important element of controlling the money supply is therefore control of the banksí ability to create deposits.

It will be recalled from Chapter 10 that an increase in the government's budget deficit implies an increase in the public sector borrowing requirement (PSBR). The PSBR is financed by borrowing through the sale of gilts to the public and by the taking up of short term public sector debt (bills) by the banks which increases the asset base of the banks as these securities constitute bank reserve assets.

This enables the banks to undertake the multiple expansion of credit, which represents an increase in M4; the majority of which is comprised of bank deposits. Figure 16.1 illustrates the link between government expenditure and the money supply.

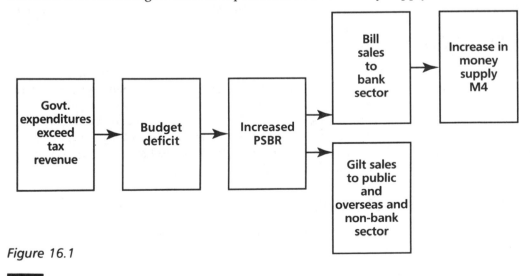

Figure 16.1

The government may attempt to sell as much of its debt as possible outside the banking system, to the public or other financial institutions, but in order to do this it will have to increase interest rates in order to attract them. To prevent an increase in the money supply by this method therefore implies a higher level of interest rates.

6 The natural rate of unemployment

Monetarists consider that the main reason for the increase in the money supply, and therefore inflation, is the commitment of governments to full employment. Governments have attempted to keep unemployment below the **'natural rate' of unemployment** (see Chapter 17) and in order to achieve this have incurred ever increasing budget deficits, with the consequent growth in the money supply. Any attempt to keep unemployment below the natural rate will therefore result in ever increasing inflation (see Chapter 17).

7 The quantity theory of money

Essentially the monetarist view represents a return to the **quantity theory of money** (see Chapter 9). It will be recalled that the quantity theory stated that

$$MV = PT$$

where M = Money supply
V = the velocity (or speed) of circulation of money
P = the price level
T = the level of transactions

The level of transactions (T) can be assumed to be the equivalent of the real level of economic activity or output.

The debate between monetarists and Keynesians hinges around V, monetarists suggest it is a constant and therefore is predictable. Keynesians argue that it varies in an unpredictable manner with changes in interest rates (see liquidity preference theory, Chapter 15). If we accept the monetarist contention that V is constant then any increase in M will result in an increase in the value of PT, and monetarists argue that the effect will fall on P (the price level) rather than T (real output), and will therefore be **inflationary, i.e. excessive growth of the money supply will increase money GDP (prices) rather than real GDP (output).**

8 The Keynesian view

It will be recalled from Chapter 12 that in Keynesian economics an increase in the money supply will influence income only **indirectly** through the reduction in the interest rate stimulating investment which would raise income through the multiplier effect. If there were unemployed resources in the economy output and real income would be raised; if there was full employment the price level would increase. In Keynesian economics therefore changes in the money supply affect the economy in an unpredictable and indirect manner and is therefore not a good policy instrument.

9 The transmission mechanism

The monetarist transmission mechanism through which increases in the money supply result in higher expenditure is quite straightforward. Money is considered to be an imperfect substitute for other financial assets and is held for its own sake. When there is an increase in the money stock the immediate effect is that people find they are holding higher money balances in relation to their holdings of other assets than they desire. They therefore attempt to reduce their money balances and increase their holdings of other assets – a kind of 'portfolio' adjustment. Some of these additional money balances will be used to purchase other forms of financial assets; however, some will be used to purchase goods and services which are also considered to yield a return to the purchaser. The increased expenditures will result in higher prices.

10 Monetarist views

Monetarists believe that fiscal policy is a destabilising influence on the economy and should be avoided. This is because of the long and variable time lags between the implementation of a policy and its effect upon the economy. For example, a reflationary policy taken during recession may take two years to take effect, by which time the economy may be growing autonomously and the effect of the policy becomes inflationary. In Figure 16.2 the trade cycle the economy would follow with no intervention is indicated by the continuous line, the broken line indicates the pro-cyclical effect of government intervention in the monetarist version.

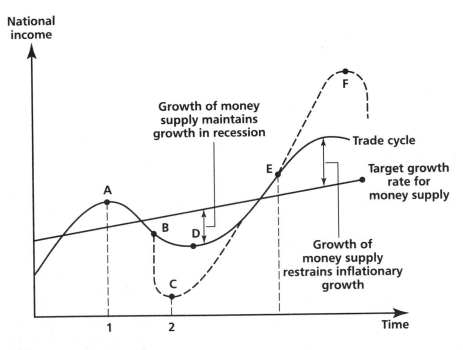

Figure 16.2

For example, the economy is on the growth or 'boom' stage of the cycle and anti-cyclical measures are taken at time period 1 to dampen down any inflationary growth tendencies. These measures do not come into effect until point B when the economy was on the down-turn anyway causing the recession to go deeper, to point C, than it would have done in the absence of such intervention, i.e. point D. Reflationary measures taken at C in time period 2 come into effect, after say 18 months, at point E when the economy is in the up-turn causing an inflationary period of excess growth to point F, and so on in a pro-cyclical manner exaggerating the upswings and downswings, rather than dampening them down in the anti-cyclical manner intended.

They believe that intervention in the economy should be minimal and that a simple monetary rule should be followed. A target rate of growth for the money supply should be announced which is consistent with the rate of growth of real output (GDP), illustrated in Figure 16.2. Attempts by the workforce to gain wage increases which are not consistent with the rate of growth of the money supply can only result in higher unemployment. Workers are expected to learn from their experiences and as reduced monetary targets are announced they will revise their expectations of inflation downwards and settle for lower wage increases. The slow growth in the money supply is sufficient to maintain growth during the down-turns in the economy and restrain inflationary or excess growth in the up-turn. Eventually the economy should stabilise around its 'natural growth rate.

11 The medium term financial strategy

Table 16.1		
	PSBR (£bn)	PSBR as a percentage of GDP
1984/5	10.2	3.1
1985/6	6.8	2.0
1986/7	3.4	0.85
1987/8	–3.0	–0.75
1988/9	–14.5	–3.0
1989/90	–7.8	–1.5
1990/1	–0.8	0.1
1991/2	13.8	2.2
1992/3	36.3	6.0
1993/4	45.4	7.0
1994/5	34.4	5.2
1995/6	21.5	4.5
1996/7	23.8 (f)	3.5 (f)

(f = forecast)
Note that a negative PSBR implies a budget surplus

The 1979 Conservative government embraced the monetarist doctrine which was embodied within the 1980 **medium term financial strategy (MTFS)**. The MTFS contained two key elements:

- A set of declining targets over a four year period for the growth of £M3.
- A plan for the reduction of the PSBR as a proportion of GDP from 4.8% in 1979/80 to 1.5% by 1983/84.

Little success was achieved in hitting the targets for the broad monetary aggregates however the attempt to reduce the PSBR as a percentage of GDP met with more success with a budget surplus being attained by 1987/88.

The stages in the development of the MTFS are summarised in Appendix 1.

The implication of the adoption of the MTFS was a switch of emphasis away from maintaining full employment to the control of inflation. The effect of the policy was thought to be more expensive in terms of unemployment the more slowly workers revise their expectations of inflation, and therefore wage demands, downwards in the light of announced targets for monetary growth. In this context it is important that the government should be seen to be achieving its targets, which is not easy given the nature of broad aggregates such as M3 and M4.

12 Criticisms of the MTFS

- One of the major criticisms of this strategy is that reductions in the money supply fall not on the price level (P) but on real output (T). The resulting decline in real output and activity results in high unemployment. It is this induced recession which critics suggest controls the price level rather than by any direct effect of the money supply on prices.
- The results of research, such as that of Friedman, is criticised because the demonstration of a close correlation between the money supply and changes in GDP is not necessarily causal, and if GDP was growing the money supply could be expected to grow in line with it.
- Keynesians suggest that if GDP is growing, attempts to control the money supply will be by-passed by the development of alternative forms of money.
- The empirical research of Friedman and Schwartz for the UK economy has been criticised by Hendry (D.F.) in an article published by the Bank of England[1]. Hendry suggests that Friedman's research in dealing with statistical evidence shows a lack of rigour and that his assertions are 'devoid of empirical support.'

13 Monetarist recommendations

Monetarists advocate a reduced role for the state:

- They believe that intervention through Keynesian type demand management policies are ineffective in reducing unemployment and result in inflation.
- The production of as many goods and services as possible should be carried out by the private sector which is believed to be more efficient and more able to respond to consumers' needs.

---

[1]Assertion Without Empirical Basis: An Econometric appraisal of *Monetary Trends in the United Kingdom* – M. Friedman and A. Schwarz. By David F. Hendry and Neil R. Ericsson. (B. of E.)

14 The monetarist experiment

In the UK the Conservative government which took power in 1979 embraced the monetarist doctrine which found expression in the medium term financial strategy, which as stated above, set targets for monetary growth and in order to secure these it was necessary to contain the level of public expenditure in real terms. The objectives of this policy were firstly the control of inflation and secondly to reduce the proportion of the economy's resources consumed by the state sector, ie to prevent the state from 'crowding out' private production. By 1987 a degree of success could be claimed in the control of inflation, however, much of the impact of monetary policy seemed to have fallen on the level of output and employment. The size of the public sector had been reduced, standing at about 45% of GDP, a figure comparable with many other industrialised nations. The use of public expenditure targets expressed in cash terms however, in order to constrain the growth of public spending in real terms, became discredited as targets were persistently overshot. Public expenditure also rose faster than expected due to public demand for better health services, education, welfare benefits and law and order, as living standards rose. Instead of aiming to cut public expenditure the 1986 Autumn Statement from the Treasury (and in the 1987 Public Expenditure White Paper Cm 56) stated that the objective was to reduce public spending as a proportion of national income, which clearly implied that an increase in real terms was acceptable provided that it was less than the rise in real GDP. This change of emphasis together with the virtual abandonment of targets for monetary growth was taken by many commentators to mean the end of the Monetarist experiment in the U.K.

Following the 1988 budget the broad monetary aggregates were abandoned for targeting purposes as the outcomes were seldom within the targeted range and the narrower definition M0 was adopted as the main monetary indicator. The rise in inflation to 8% during 1989/90 resulted in a tightening of monetary policy but with reliance on interest rates as the main policy instrument; interest rates rising to 15% by the end of 1989. The economy was slow to respond to the rise in interest rates and the increase worsened the recession. Monetary policy was relaxed in 1991 as interest rates fell to 10.5% with further decreases in 1992 to 7% and 1993 to 6.5%.

In 1993 the government specified a range of 3–9% for maintaining the growth of M4. Interest rates rose in 1995 only to fall again in 1996 to below 6%.

Self assessment questions

1 What is meant by 'taxation without representation'?

2 Describe how an increase in the PSBR implies an increase in the money supply.

3 How is the commitment to 'full employment' connected with increases in the PSBR?

4 What assumptions are implied by monetarists regarding the velocity of circulation of money (V)?

5 Outline the monetarist transmission mechanism by which increases in the money supply result in higher expenditures and prices.

6 Outline the monetarist rule for the growth of the money supply.

7 Why was is it considered necessary to announce targets for monetary growth?

8 Why have governments experienced difficulty in achieving targets set for the growth of broad monetary aggregates?

Appendix 1

The medium term financial strategy (MTFS) was introduced in 1980 in the belief that by setting targets for the growth of the money supply, the money supply, and therefore inflation, could be controlled. Targeting the money supply however proved to be far more difficult in practice, largely because there is no unique definition of money and furthermore there is no means by which the money supply can be directly controlled. Since its introduction therefore the exact nature of the MTFS has frequently been changed. Targeting the money supply is one thing but hitting the target is another. When the government responded by changing the target many commentators accused them of resorting to 'moving the goal posts'. Targets for the growth of the money supply have been expressed in various forms since 1980, but can be summarised as follows:

1980-82   The only target was sterling M3 (£M3)

1982-84   M1, £M3 and PSL2

1984–88   MO and £M3

1988–90   MO only

1993–present   M0 and M4

The measures of money published by the Bank of England have also changed over the period, and the only measures now published (June 1990) are as follows (read in conjunction with Chapter 10):

MO   Cash in circulation plus commercial bank operational deposits at the Bank of England

N1B M1   Cash in circulation plus non-interest bearing private sector sight deposits with banks

M2   Cash in circulation plus retail deposits with banks, building societies and the National Savings Bank

M4   Cash in circulation plus all private sector sterling bank and building society deposits

M5   M4 plus private holdings of money market instruments and national savings instruments

The exercise has lost much of its credibility because, as indicated above, when monetary targets do not behave as the government wishes them to they are simply replaced by different targets or their importance is reduced by taking into consideration some other indicators. For example, the Chancellor said in his 1984 budget speech that he would 'take account of other indicators of broad money in particular PSL2'. It was just as well that PSL2 was not targeted because it grew by 14.4% over the year.

During the first 3 months of the 1985 target period £M3 grew by 4.4% which is an annual rate of 19%. The immediate reaction to the overshoot was to announce in the Economic Progress Report May 1985 that the presentation of the figures would be changed.

The change is in fact entirely sensible but the timing was unfortunate and it does seem that overshoots are no longer regarded with alarm; the government merely tries to present the figures in as palatable a way as possible. The change actually reduced the growth in £M3 from 19% to 12% which was still 3% above the target. In a highly significant speech at Loughborough University on 22nd October 1986 the Governor of the Bank of England, Mr. Leigh-Pemberton questioned the ability of governments to control M3 and therefore the usefulness of setting broad monetary targets, 'which may even become counter productive serving to undermine confidence .... '

By 1988 targeting for the broad monetary aggregate had been abandoned and the March 1988 budget contained a target for the narrow definition M0 only. The key points of the MTFS announced in the 1988 budget were as follows:

- The broad aim of policy is the steady reduction of inflation, over the medium term, by reducing the growth of total spending power in the economy, as measured by the cash value of national output (money GDP).
- The growth of M0 to be kept within the range 1–5% in 1988-9.
- Interest rate decisions to be based on a continuous and comprehensive assessment of monetary conditions to maintain downward pressure on inflation.
- A balanced budget to be the norm, for the medium term.

The actual trends for M0, M4, GDP and the PSBR are shown below

TABLE 1

MONEY GDP, MONEY SUPPLY AND THE PSBR

Year	90–91	91–92	92–93	93–94	94–95
Money GDP[1]	4.2	4.5	4.2	6.0	5.3
M0[2]	3.0	2.5	5.6	7.3	5.2
PSBR[3]	−0.6	13.8	36.3	45.4	35.9
M4[4]	5.8	3.6	4.6	4.6	9.9

[1] Percentage change on previous year.
[2] and [4] percentage change on previous year.
[3] £ billion, cash.

Appendix 2

The monetarist consumption function and the permanent income hypothesis

This appendix is optional for A level students but would be useful to more advanced students.

The permanent income hypothesis

Post-war cross sectional data on the consumption function has consistently provided a poor fit to that forecast on the basis of long-run time series data. Friedman's **permanent**

income hypothesis provides one possible solution to this problem. The central theme of Friedman's theory is that **planned or permanent consumption** is proportional to expected or **permanent income**. Permanent income itself is dependent upon the individual's stock of wealth and subjective rate of interest (not market rate). Permanent income can be viewed as the annual flow of income generated by the individual's estimated stock of wealth at a rate equal to the rate of interest. Alternatively, it is the annual flow of resources that could be spent by the individual without disturbing his estimated stock of wealth. Both permanent income and permanent consumption differ from measured income and consumption by amounts Friedman calls **transitory income** and **transitory consumption**. Current measured consumption (C) is the sum of transitory consumption (CT) and permanent consumption (CP), and current measured income (Y) is the sum of transitory income (YT) and permanent income (YP). The relation can be summarised as

(Measured) $C = CP + CT$
(Measured) $Y = YP + YT$
$CP = kYP$ (k = factor of proportionality)

Friedman also assumes that there is no systematic relationship or correlation between permanent income and transitory income, between consumption and transitory consumption.

Monetarist consumption function

Friedman's version of the consumption function therefore differs significantly from the simple relationship between consumption and disposable income described in Chapter 12. In this version of the consumption function consumption depends upon total resources available. Resources are assumed to include income from non-human wealth (i.e. property) plus income from human wealth (future earnings). The relationship described above between permanent consumption (CP) and permanent income (YP) is the basis of the consumption function which can be summarised in the equation:

$CP = k (i, w, u) YP$

- The subjective rate of interest, i, at which the consumer can borrow or lend (not the market rate)
- The relative importance of property and non property income, symbolised by the ratio of non-human wealth to income (w)and
- The factors symbolised by the portmanteau variable u determining the consumer's tastes and preferences for consumption versus additions to wealth.

Consumption here refers to the **flow of services** which goods yield over their lifetime, not the initial expenditure, since utility is derived from their services, not from the expenditure. For example a refrigerator will yield a service to the purchaser over its lifetime, say 10 years; in this sense it is therefore 'consumed' over 10 years.

The essential point is that changes in income that are believed to be temporary do not cause the individual to revise his estimates of permanent income. Also unexpected or transitory changes in consumption spending cause no alteration or modification to permanent consumption expenditures.

The MPC out of transitory income is zero.

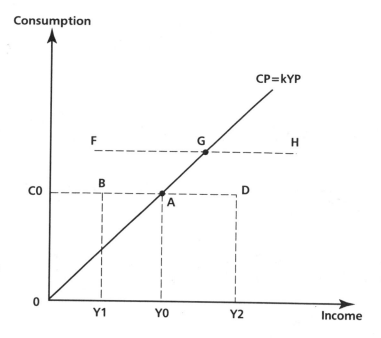

Figure 16.3

Transitory income

The implication is that sudden or 'windfall' changes as a result of government fiscal policy may not have the predicted effect upon levels of consumption. Thus the multiplier effect of a tax reduction will be much lower than originally thought (or zero). The concept of transitory income provides one explanation for the poor fit of post-war consumption data to estimated consumption. This is illustrated in Figure 16.3.

Permanent consumption function is plotted through the origin, i.e. CP. Suppose income falls from Y0 to Y1 and households perceive this fall to be transitory with no change in YP. Since there is no correlation between CT and YT and because permanent income has not changed, measured consumption will therefore not change. Thus for the fall in measured income from Y0 to Y 1 measured consumption remains constant at C0. The same is true of an increase Y0 to Y2, giving the same consumption C0. Observed points from data would trace the line BAD. A consumption function fitted to these observations would not be the 'true' consumption-function. An increase in income which persisted long enough to be considered as permanent would result in a move from A to G, but there would then be a new 'short run' consumption function FGH. Successive points such as A and G produce the long run consumption function. The discrepancy between long run and short run observations is therefore explained by the fact that cross section, or short run data are observing short run consumption functions as BAD and FGH, whilst long run data are observing points such as A and G on the long run function.

17

The natural rate of unemployment and the Phillips curve

1 The monetarist view

The concept of the **natural rate of unemployment** is closely associated with the monetarist school of thought, and has much in common with the classical view of the labour market. It differs from the Keynesian view in that it considers unemployment from the **supply** side of the economy rather than as resulting from deficient demand.

2 The labour market

The labour market is considered to be like any other market where the equilibrium price, which in this instance is the wage rate, is determined by demand and supply. The amount of labour demanded by employers will depend upon the level of real wages.

$$\text{Real wages} = \frac{\text{Money wages}}{\text{Prices}} = \left(\frac{W}{P}\right)$$

The higher the real wage the lower the demand for labour, and vice versa. The total supply of labour will increase as the real wage rises and fall as the real wage falls. Provided the market operates smoothly then an equilibrium real wage will be established where the demand and supply for labour is equal. Any unemployment remaining when the labour market is in equilibrium is referred to as the **natural rate of unemployment.**

In Figure 17.1 DD is the demand curve for labour which slopes downwards reflecting the declining marginal productivity of labour. SL is the supply curve which slopes upwards indicating that at higher real wages more labour will be supplied. The labour market is in equilibrium at E with real wage $(W/P)^2$ and QL^E labour. If the real wage was above the equilibrium wage, for example at $(W/P)^1$ the quantity of labour demanded would fall to QL^1 but QL^2 would be supplied, there is therefore an excess supply of labour at this higher real wage and QL^1–QL^2 will be unemployed at the prevailing real wage rate. Full employment could be restored by reducing real wages, for example by cutting money wages, this would increase the demand for labour and eliminate some of the excess supply returning the labour market to equilibrium at E. The implication is that unemployment such as QL^1–QL^2 is caused by real wages being too high and therefore the cure is to accept cuts in real wages. It follows therefore that any unemployment existing at the employment level QL^E is **voluntary** and occurs because workers are not willing to work for a low enough wage. The residual unemployment that exists at the equilibrium employment level QL^E is referred to as the **natural rate of unemployment** and is the unemployment which remains when the labour market is in equilibrium.

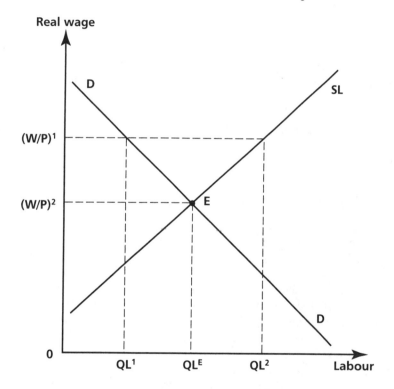

Figure 17.1

Advocates of the natural rate consider that full employment as defined in the post-war era (3% in the UK) was a political objective rather than an economic concept. The natural rate of unemployment is the level the labour market would tend towards if wages were flexible and in the absence of artificial 'frictions' or obstacles.

3 The natural rate of unemployment

The natural rate of unemployment cannot be defined as some percentage of the labour force as it is not a constant. It depends upon a number of factors which are liable to change:

- Technology and innovation.
- Comparative advantage and international trade.
- The degree of occupational and geographical mobility.
- Information regarding job opportunities.
- Restrictive practices imposed by trade unions.

4 Frictions in the labour market

If unemployment is persistently high and above what may be considered the natural rate, according to this theory it is because the labour market is being prevented from operating smoothly and efficiently by the existence of 'frictions' or obstacles to supply. There are two main sources of such frictions which are suggested:

- The high level of benefit paid to the unemployed which prevents them from taking low paid jobs. Professor Minford suggests a combination of reduced benefits and lower taxation as an incentive to the unemployed to take lower paid jobs. He suggests this disincentive effect is felt most strongly in the non-unionised sector of the workforce.
- The power of trade unions to resist reductions in real wages and impose minimum wage rates prevents people from obtaining jobs at lower pay which they might otherwise take.
- Both are areas which are highly controversial politically.

5 Breakdown of the Phillips curve

Monetarists suggest that any attempt by governments to keep the level of unemployment below the natural rate will result in ever accelerating inflation. This has important implications for the Phillips Curve which it will be recalled from Chapter 13 implied a stable 'trade-off' between prices and employment. Governments could select a level of inflation and engineer the appropriate level of unemployment. However the Phillips curve relationship started to break down towards the end of the 1960s and by the mid 1970s seemed to have broken down altogether, underpredicting the inflation rate by about 20%. Table 17.1 shows the change in retail prices and unemployment over the period 1962 to 1995.

By 1976 instead of 5% unemployment giving the predicted wage stability it was associated with inflation of almost 25%. It was possible that the relationship had broken down altogether. An alternative suggestion was that the curve had shifted to the right, to PC2 in Figure 17.2, so that 5½% unemployment was now associated with 25% inflation, and stable wages would now only be achieved at much higher levels of unemployment, such as y.

The implication is that policies designed to stabilise inflation by reducing expenditure would now result in much higher unemployment levels than previously. Various reasons have been put forward for this apparent breakdown in the Phillips curve relationship but the fact that governments resorted to incomes policies at that time would suggest that they considered that wages and therefore costs were the most important factor. The view

Footnote to Table opposite:
[1]. The basis of compilation of unemployment statistics was changed in March 1986 reducing the figure by approximately 50,000.

TABLE 17.1		
Year	Unemployment (UK Excl. N. Ireland)	Change in Retail Prices (%)
62	1.8	2.6
63	2.2	2.1
64	1.6	3.3
65	1.3	4.8
66	1.4	3.9
67	2.2	2.5
68	2.3	4.7
69	2.3	5.4 (Av 3.53)
70	2.5	6.4
71	3.3	9.4
72	3.6	7.1
73	2.6	9.2
74	2.5	16.1
75	3.9	24.2
76	5.2	16.5
77	5.7	15.8
78	5.6	8.3
79	5.3	13.4 (Av 12.4)
80	6.7	18.0
81	10.4	11.9
82	11.7	8.6
83	12.4	4.6
84	12.6	5.0
85	13.1	6.1
86	11.41	3.4
87	10.0	4.1
88	7.8	4.9
89	6.0	7.8 (Av 7.44)
90	5.6	9.5
91	7.9	5.9
92	9.6	3.7
93	10.2	1.6
94	9.3	2.5
95	8.2	3.4 (Av 4.43)

that cost increases were responsible operates within the traditional framework of the Phillips curve and has two main elements:

The first is that prices rose due to cost-push inflation. This was associated with an increase in trade union militancy whereby trade unions were able to gain pay increases for their members which were greater than the rate of increase of productivity. Firms' costs would then rise and as a consequence prices would also rise. The increase in prices would reduce demand, resulting in increased unemployment and the simultaneous rise in prices and unemployment implies a worsening of the terms of the trade-off, and therefore the shift to the right of the curve to PC2 (Figure 17.2). If the government then attempts to increase aggregate demand in order to reduce unemployment there will be a further rise in inflation from a point such as x in Figure 17.2 to a point such as z with its high rate of inflation. This explanation sees the ability of trade unions to gain wage increases for their members above the rate of productivity increase even when unemployment is high, and the market power of firms to pass on these increases as being the main reason for the shift.

This explanation also incorporates the external cost increases, such as the oil price rises and the commodity price boom of 1970s, as being of major significance in the process.

It also includes the possibility of higher benefits making the unemployed more selective about which jobs they take and an unwillingness to accept the lowest paid jobs.

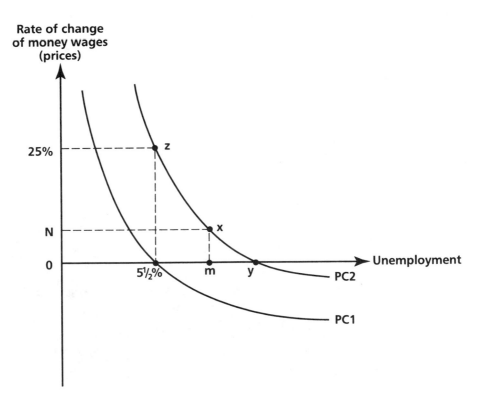

Figure 17.2

6 Expectations

Friedman criticised the original Phillips curve on the grounds that it assumed that the **anticipated** rate of inflation was given, and also that the effect of **expectations** on inflation had been omitted; in which case the stable Phillips curve relationship was only a very **short-run phenomenon**. In the longer run there was no stable relationship and **any attempts by government to reduce unemployment below the natural rate would result in accelerating inflation and the return of unemployment to the natural rate.** The orthodox Phillips curve assumes that workers suffer from a 'money illusion', i.e. the belief that an increase in money wages is the same as an increase in real wages. However if we assume that workers learn from their past experiences of rising prices they will begin to base their behaviour on what they **anticipate** the rate of inflation to be and begin to bargain in **real** terms, i.e. they see through the money illusion. Workers will only offer themselves for employment if they believe their **real wage** will rise. The greater the anticipated rate of inflation the greater the increase in **money** wages workers will demand in order to maintain the value of their real wage.

7 Long run Phillips curve

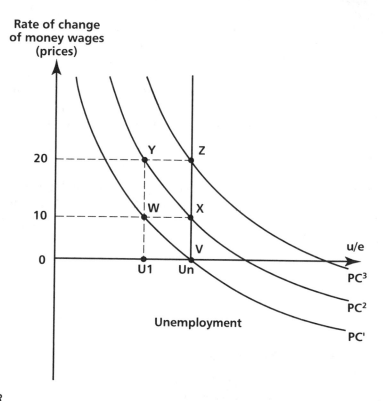

Figure 17.3

According to Friedman the long run Phillips curve is **vertical** at the **natural rate of unemployment,** i.e. there is no long run trade-off between inflation and unemployment.

For each level of anticipated inflation there will be a different Phillips curve. In Figure 17.3 the three curves indicated represent different expected inflation rates. Un represents the natural rate of unemployment. If the government believes this rate of unemployment to be too high and attempts to reduce it to Ul by expansionary fiscal and monetary policies the economy moves to point W with 10% inflation. This increase in the price level reduces real wages making labour more attractive so firms employ additional labour and expand output and then pass on the wage increase in the form of higher prices. The workers accepting employment did so because they believed their real wages had risen. At point W however they realise that they have over estimated the increase in their real wage. As workers experience the 10% inflation rate they begin to anticipate inflation of 10% and the Phillips curve shifts to the right to PC2 which is consistent with 10% inflation. As workers are interested only in the **real wage** and this has now fallen due to inflation to what it was originally, unemployment returns to the natural rate at point X as workers leave those jobs where the real wage has not risen and search for jobs with a higher real wage. At point X inflation is 10% and unemployment has returned to Un. At X if the government wishes to reduce unemployment again to Ul by expanding demand it will result in a 20% inflation rate at point Y and then shift to PC3 as workers learn to anticipate a 20% inflation rate. Again the same process is followed with a return to the natural rate at Z, the same level of unemployment but with a 20% rate of inflation. There is therefore no long term trade-off, workers are temporarily 'fooled' into thinking their real wages have risen by governments pursuing expansionary policies, but unemployment returns to the natural rate accompanied by accelerating inflation. The 'actual' Phillips curve is the vertical line V–Z. The implication being that in the long run that governments cannot permanently reduce unemployment below the natural rate by using fiscal and monetary policy, it can however have a choice of the rate of inflation, which will be stable at the natural rate. The incorporation of expectations into the analysis provides one explanation of the observed behaviour of the Phillips curve.

8 Adaptive expectations

The way in which people formed their expectations in the previous analysis suggests that people's adjustments to rising prices takes time. This implies that they form their expectations about future prices by projecting their past experience of **actual prices**, with most weight being given to the most recent past, i.e. it is a model which contains a series of lagged responses with declining weights given to the responses as they are more distant in time. It is therefore referred to as the **adaptive expectations** model. This approach does allow for the possibility of demand management policies if the size of the lags could be estimated and appropriate weights selected, although Friedman would suggest that this possibility was unlikely because of the extreme variability of the lagged responses.

9 Rational expectations

A third school of economic thought developed in the 1970s, the new classical (or neo classical) economists. The new classical economists take a more extreme view than the monetarists regarding the ability of governments to influence the level of economic activity through stabilisation policies. The central tenet of their argument is that real variables such as output and employment cannot be influenced by systematic demand management policies in either short-run or the long-run, and they include both **fiscal** and monetary policy measures in this conclusion. Stabilisation measures of either a fiscal or monetary nature are incapable of influencing either employment or output. This conclusion is based upon the rejection by the new classical economists of the way in which price expectations are formed in both the Keynesian model and the adaptive expectations model of the monetarists. These formulations of price expectations are rejected because they both assume that expectations in the labour market of current and future price levels are based solely upon past experience of price levels. This assumption is criticised as being naïve in the extreme and they ask why should rational economic agents forming an expectation of future price levels rely only upon past levels of prices, and particularly if such behaviour resulted in them being systematically in error whenever there is a shift in aggregate demand – from the point of view that they will persistently fail to realise that such shifts are accompanied by increases in the price level? If people operate on this basis then they are going to be systematically in error which is clearly not rational. Putting it simply, people generally learn from their experience so there is no reason not to expect them to do so in the labour market.

The new classical economists propose **a rational expectations model** which suggests that when people form views about the future they will take into account **all available information** regarding the variable being predicted, and will use this information intelligently, i.e. they will understand the effect of this information on the variable they are attempting to predict. In particular they will understand the relationship between demand management policies and the price level and will adjust their behaviour accordingly. For example, if the government systematically reacts to an increase in unemployment by expansionary fiscal and monetary policies people will anticipate the increase in prices and the effect of budget deficit on future interest rates and taxes, and adjust their own consumption behaviour to accommodate them, thus making ineffective the policy measures. Although individuals are assumed to be rational however, the model does not preclude the possibility of them not having perfect information and where they do have imperfect information they may make mistakes in predicting the price level and such mistakes may cause short-run deviations in output and employment from the natural rate which would exist with full information. This would be the case for any unanticipated changes in the level of demand, the implication is however that the effects of any systematic policy measure by government will be anticipated and will be wholly ineffective as a consequence. The rational expectations model therefore casts severe doubts upon the effectiveness of demand management policies.

10 Supply-side economics

The **new classical** economists stress the importance of **supply factors** in determining the growth of output. As discussed above, these economists cast doubt upon the ability of changes in aggregate demand to significantly change output and employment. These economists, sometimes referred to as **supply side** economists, accept the classical view that output is determined by **real variables** and therefore **stress the importance of the growth of supply of the factors of production** and **technological change**. They also place more emphasis on the **role of interest rates in investment**. Supply side economists, like the classical economists, also stress the superiority of the **free-market system** and believe that **government intervention** in the economy should be reduced to a **minimum**. The main points in the **supply side** argument are as follows:

- The growth of output is mainly determined by the **growth of the supply of the factors of production and technological change.**
- The supply of labour is affected significantly by the **incentive to work,** in particular the post-tax real wage, hence they stress the importance of rates of personal taxation and benefits. In the long-run changes in population are also important.
- The **supply of capital** is determined by the incentives to save and invest, in particular the **post-tax returns** to **saving and investment.** In this instance they stress the importance of **rates of interest** and **personal and corporate taxation.**
- **Government intervention** in business activity through regulations and taxation has **reduced investment** and **labour productivity,** and therefore growth of output has been lower than it would otherwise have been.

11 Fiscal drag

Supply side economists are opposed to attempts to achieve higher growth rates through the expansion of aggregate demand in the Keynesian manner. They suggest that such policies may actually reduce growth because the inflation which it generates reduces the return from investment and the incentive to work. The incentive to work is reduced by the combined effects of inflation and progressive taxation. As nominal (money) incomes rise due to inflation the income recipient is moved into a higher tax bracket (or into taxation). At the same time as the tax liability is increased the real income may be unchanged, or even be lower, resulting in a reduction in real post-tax income. The consequence of this **fiscal drag** is a reduction in the incentive to work. In order to reduce this dis-incentive to work a combination of lower benefits and lower direct taxation is suggested (see Frictions in the labour market; paragraph 4).

Self assessment questions

1 Account for the apparent shift in the Phillips curve which took place in the 1970s.

2 Why is 'money illusion' necessary for the operation of the orthodox Phillips curve?

3 Outline the relationship between the natural rate of unemployment and inflation.

4 What is the rational expectations model and why does it cast doubt on the effectiveness of demand management policies?

5 What factors do the new classical economists stress as important in determining the rate of growth of output?

6 What is fiscal drag?

18

The IS-LM and aggregate demand/supply models

1 Real and money sectors

The methods used to analyse national income, in particular the use of 45° lines and the aggregate demand curve, are subject to the criticism that they ignore the monetary and assets sector of the economy. The IS–LM model attempts to overcome this by incorporating both the **real** and **monetary** sectors. (This Chapter may be considered as optional by professional and 'A' level students but the model is becoming more widely used as a tool of analysis and would be necessary reading for undergraduate students).

2 The IS curve

The IS function represents the **real** sector of the economy, i.e. goods and services, and the **IS curve** indicates the combinations of **national income and interest rates at which desired investment demand is equal to desired savings.**

The IS curve can be derived algebraically or geometrically. Figure 18.1 illustrates the geometrical derivation using four quadrants. The analysis assumes all prices are constant, with a closed economy.

Figure 18.1 consists of four quadrants which are read anti-clockwise, from 18.1(a) to 18.1(d).

Quadrant 18.1(a) relates the quantity of investment to the rate of interest and is therefore the demand curve for capital, or marginal efficiency of capital curve (see Chapter 15).

In Quadrant 18.1(b) the 45° line represents the equilibrium condition for the closed economy, derived in Chapter 12, of **saving = investment (S = I)**. The horizontal axis measures the amount of investment demand corresponding with that in 18.1(a) and the appropriate amount of savings for equilibrium can be identified by reading it off from the 45° line, as the 45° line will produce an equal reading on both axes.

Quadrant 18.1(c) incorporates the savings function derived in Chapter 12. Savings are assumed to be positively related to income so the savings function slopes upwards, the steepness of the slope being dependent upon the marginal propensity to save. The equilibrium quantity of savings is projected from 18.1(b) to 18.1(c) where the level of national income necessary to generate the required level of saving for equilibrium can be established.

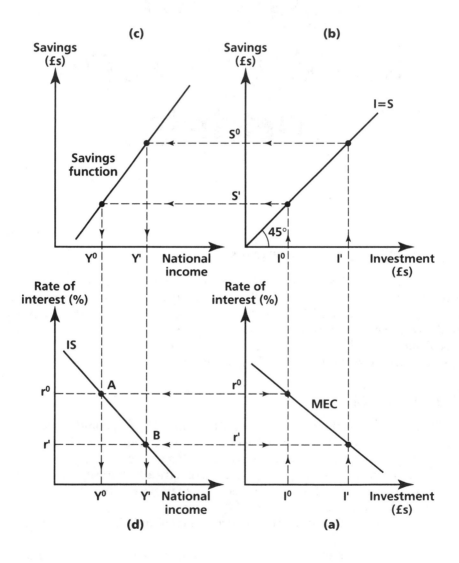

Figure 18.1

Quadrant 18.1(d) shows the derivation of the IS curve. The horizontal axis shows national income and corresponds with that in quadrant 18.1(c). Projecting down from 18.1(c) to 18.1(d) and where this coincides with the appropriate rate of interest from 18.1(a) produces one unique point on the IS curve where the combination of the rate of interest and national income will produce equality between desired saving and desired investment. By sequentially deriving numerous points such as A and B the IS curve can be derived.

3 Adjustments to the IS curve

Government expenditure can easily be incorporated into the model by horizontally adding it to the MEC curve in quadrant 18.I(a) and shifting the curve to the right, i.e. I + G.

In order to incorporate taxation a similar adjustment is made to the savings function in 18.1(c), where taxation shifts the curve to the left, i.e. S + T.

In neither case is the fundamental analysis altered, and the IS curve will be assumed here to incorporate both government expenditure and taxation.

4 The slope of the curve

The **steepness** of the **slope** of the IS curve is determined by:

- The **interest elasticity** (sensitivity) of **investment**. The more sensitive is investment to the rate of interest the **flatter** is the IS curve.
- The **marginal propensity to save (MPS)**. The higher the MPS the steeper the IS curve.

5 Shifts in the IS curve

Shifts in the IS curve result from:

- Changes in **government expenditure**. An **increase** in government expenditure will shift the IS curve to the **right**, and a **reduction** to the **left.**
- Changes in the **rate of income tax.** An **increase** in tax will shift the curve to the **left**, and a **reduction** to the **right**.

6 The real sector

The IS curve **represents the real,** or **goods and services sector of the economy,** and as it represents equilibrium then the aggregate demand for goods and services will be equal to aggregate supply at all points on the curve.

7 The LM curve

The LM curve represents the **monetary sector** of the economy and can also be derived by utilising a four quadrant diagram. The derivation of the LM curve is illustrated in Figure 18. 2

Quadrant 18.2(a) indicates the **demand for speculative money balances** relative to the rate of interest. The resulting relationship is downward sloping representing the inverse relationship between asset prices (bonds) and the rate of interest (see Chapter 15).

Quadrant 18.2(b) is referred to as the **money supply line.** Projecting upwards from 18.2(a) to 18.2(b) we obtain the size of speculative money balances, and if we assume that the only other significant money balances are **transactions balances**, then given a fixed supply of money the difference must be the **transactions balances** which can be identi-fied on the vertical axis of 18.2(b). The greater the speculative balances the smaller are the transactions balances and vice versa and the sum of the two will be equal to the fixed money supply as the line intersects both axes at the same total value. It therefore indicates the distribution of the money supply between the two types of money balance, and given the level of speculative balances in 18.2(a) it indicates the level of demand for real trans-actions balances which is consistent with monetary equilibrium.

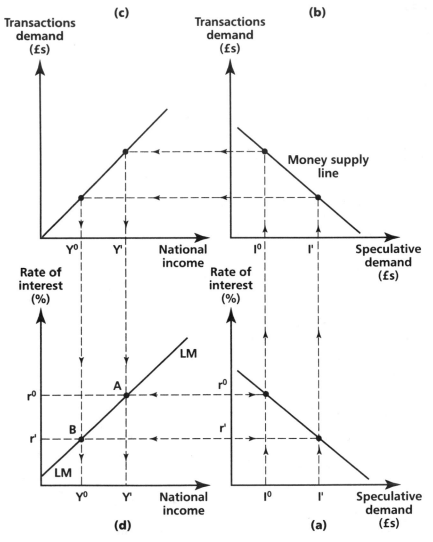

Figure 18.2

Projecting this level of transaction demand horizontally to quadrant 18.2(c) the level of national income required to generate that level of transactions demand can be identified. The transactions demand function slopes upwards with income as these balances will need to be larger as income rises in order to maintain the larger number of transactions.

Quadrant 18.2(d) has the rate of interest on the vertical axis and national income on the horizontal axis. The level of national income from 18.2(c) is projected down and where this coincides with the appropriate rate of interest a single point on the LM curve is identified. Starting with different interest rates and following the process around the quadrants produce numerous such points which can be connected to give the LM curve.

8 The slope of the LM curve

The steepness of the **slope** of the LM curve depends upon:

- The **interest elasticity** (sensitivity) of the **speculative demand** for money. The greater the interest elasticity the flatter the curve.
- The **sensitivity** of the **transactions demand** for money to changes in national income. The more sensitive the demand the steeper the LM curve.

9 Shifts in the LM curve

Shifts in the LM curve occur as a result of changes in the **supply of money**. An increase in the money supply shifting the LM curve to the right, and reductions shifting it to the left.

10 The monetary sector

Each point on the LM curve indicates a rate of interest and level of national income for which the total demand for money is equal to the total supply of money and as such represents **equilibrium in the monetary sector.**

11 The IS-LM model

The complete IS-LM model combines both the IS and LM curves and the intersection of the two curves represents the combination of the rate of interest and national income which **simultaneously produces equilibrium in both the monetary and real sectors of the economy and therefore the economy as a whole.** This unique equilibrium point is illustrated in Figure 18.3, with interest rate r^0 and national income Y^0.

12 Fiscal and monetary policy

The IS-LM model can be used to illustrate the effects of either fiscal or monetary policy. An increase in government expenditure will have the effect of shifting the IS curve to the right. This is illustrated in Figure 18.4.

In Figure 18.4 the increase in government expenditure shifts the IS curve from IS to IS'. If we assume that the rate of interest **remains constant** then income shifts from Y^0 to Y'', this is the full multiplier effect discussed in Chapter 12. Incorporating the monetary effects of the increased expenditure indicates that the increase in income will be associated with an **increase in the interest rate**, and income will rise only to Y^1 with an increase in the interest rate to r^1. The rise in the interest rate **'crowds out'** some private expenditure and the increase in income is less than it would have been if the rate of interest had remained constant. The **'crowding out effect'** therefore **reduces the size of the multiplier.** The rise in interest rates results from:

- The need to offer higher rates of interest on government bonds in order to attract the public to buy them.
- The increased demand for money as income rises.

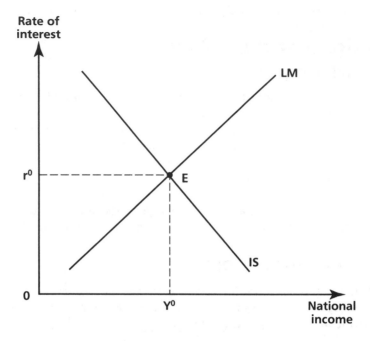

Figure 18.3

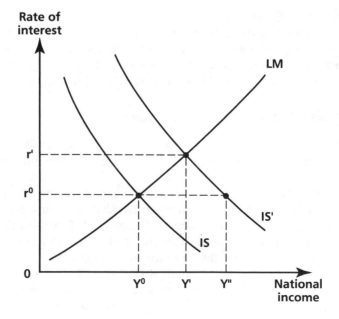

Figure 18.4

13 The wealth effect

It is also necessary to consider the affect of the change in private **wealth** which may occur as a result of a budget deficit financed by the issue of government bonds.

- A budget deficit will normally involve an increase in the holding of bonds by the public. This represents an increase in private **wealth**, which results in greater consumption out of any given income, in which case the **wealth effect** augments the multiplier effect.
- The increase in wealth however, will also have an affect on financial markets. It is argued by monetarists that where the government's deficit is financed by the issue of bonds there may be a further level of crowding out. This occurs as a result of the fall in bond prices which accompanies the rise in interest rates mentioned above. The fall in bond prices reduces the wealth of bond holders who then increase the level of their savings in order to regain their previous levels of wealth, this **wealth effect** further reduces private expenditures and dampens the multiplier effect.
- Whether the net result of these two influences is expansionary or contractionary will depend upon their relative strengths.

14 Monetary policy v fiscal policy

The debate over the advocacy of monetary policy (monetarists) relative to fiscal policy (generally Keynesians) can be analysed by utilising IS-LM curve analysis and making different assumptions about the relative slopes of the curves.

Monetarists assume that the demand for money has zero interest elasticity, i.e. is inelastic, the LM curve is therefore very steep, or vertical. Investment is assumed to be interest elastic and the IS curve therefore has a shallower slope.

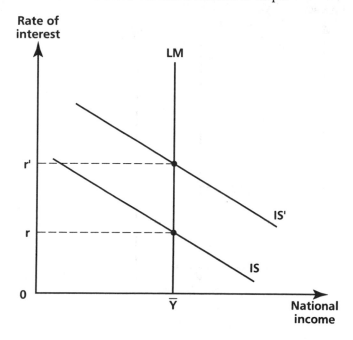

Figure 18.5

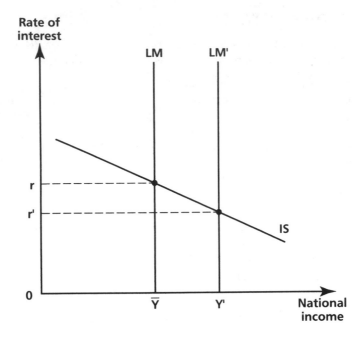

Figure 18.6

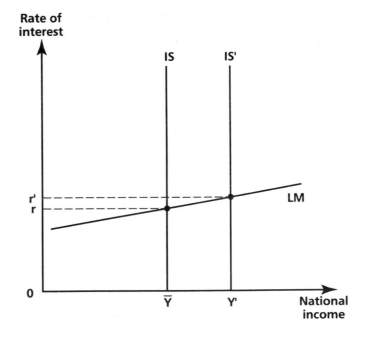

Figure 18.7

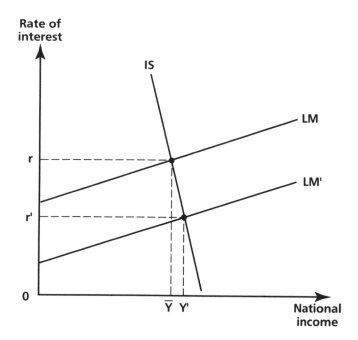

Figure 18.8

In Figure 18.5 an increase in government spending shifts the IS curve to IS' but due to the inelastic money demand income remains unchanged at Y and the impact falls upon the rate of interest which rises to r'. **fiscal policy** is **therefore ineffective**. Alternatively **increasing the money supply** as illustrated in Diagram 18.6 shifts the LM curve to the right and has a **powerful effect upon income.**

Keynesians assume that the demand for money is interest elastic (see Chapter 15) and the LM curve therefore has a shallower slope. Interest rates are assumed to have little effect upon investment demand which implies that the IS curve is steeper. The relative slopes are illustrated in Figure 18.7 and 18.8.

In Figure 18.7 an increase in government expenditure shifts the IS curve to IS' increasing income from $\bar{Y}$ to Y', **fiscal policy therefore has a powerful effect upon income.** Figure 18.8 illustrates an increase in the money supply which shifts the LM curve from LM to LM' leaving income only slightly changed at Y', the impact falling upon interest rates. **Monetary policy is therefore an ineffective policy instrument** for generating changes in income.

In the extreme case, which Keynes referred to as the liquidity trap, the demand for money becomes infinitely elastic and all increases in the money supply are held in the form of speculative money balances. This is represented by the horizontal portion of the LM curve. A–B, in Figure 18.9. In the liquidity trap increases in the money supply (LM', LM²) would be totally ineffective, and changes in income could only be brought about through the use of fiscal policy.

The interest elasticity of the demand for money is an empirical matter and there appears to be little evidence to support the extreme cases. In the 'normal' case illustrated in Diagram 18.3 both fiscal and monetary policy have a role to play.

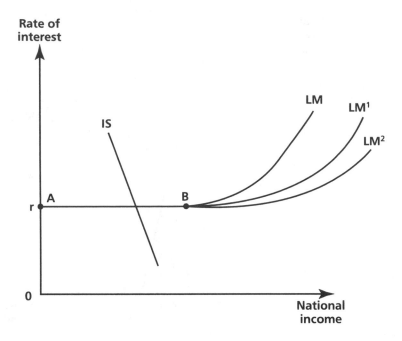

Figure 18.9

15 The aggregate demand curve

A technique which has become increasingly used as a method of macro-economic analysis is the **aggregate demand and supply model.** It is important to note here that the **aggregate demand curve** (AD curve) used in this method of analysis is not the same thing as the aggregate monetary demand (AMD) curve described in Chapter 12. The AD curve can be derived graphically from the IS-LM model, with the price level as an endogenous variable. Figure 18.10 illustrates the IS-LM model in the upper section A and in the lower section, B; the AD curve which is derived from it. The initial equilibrium level of national income is Y with interest rate r where the IS curve and LM curves intersect at E. For this analysis the money stock is held constant and the price level is allowed to vary. The LM curve is associated with the price level P, this is identified with point Z on the lower section, B, at the locus of price level P and income Y. The price level is now allowed to rise to P while the money stock is held constant, which reduces the real stock of money and thereby shifts the LM curve upwards to the left to LM'. The new equilibrium is at E' with income Y'. This can be plotted in section B to produce point W. A further rise in the price level to P^2 shifts the LM curve further to the left to LM^2, and following the same procedure point X can be derived. By following the same process numerous points such as XWZ can be identified, and by joining them together the AD curve is derived. The AD curve like the demand curve described earlier in market analysis slopes downward to the right and relates price to quantity (real national income or output). Because the AD curve is derived from the intersection of the IS-LM curves however, all the points plotted along it represent simultaneous equilibrium in both the goods and assets market, given that autonomous expenditure and the nominal money supply are held constant. Changes in either autonomous expenditure (C, I, G or X) or in the nominal money supply, will shift the AD curve; increases shifting it to the right and vice versa.

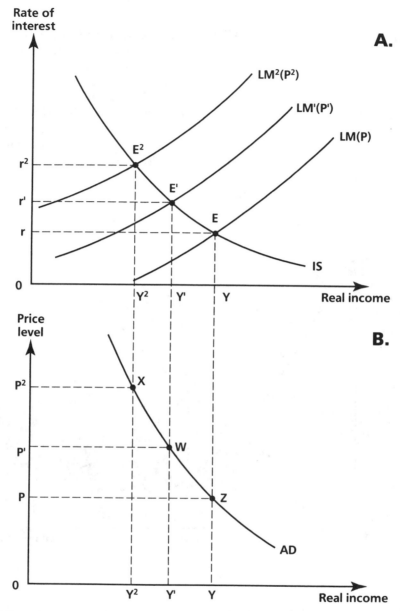

Figure 18.10

16 The aggregate supply curve

The **aggregate supply curve (AS)** is simply the relationship which exists between the price level and the amount produced in the economy. The concept is the same as that illustrated in the lower section of Figure 13.1 which related the level of output to the price level. The AS curve is assumed to slope upwards to the right as firms' marginal costs rise as output is increased.

17 Equilibrium

Figure 18.11 illustrates the combined AD and AS curves with initial equilibrium at E, with price level P and real income (output) Y. The government generates a shift in the AD curve to AD^1 by policy measures, operating on the level of demand, either a reduction in taxation, increase in government expenditure, adjusting the exchange rate, or by an increase in the nominal money stock. The shift to AD^1 raises income to Y^1 and the price level to P^1. It should be noted that the full Keynesian multiplier would have raised income to Y^2 (E–A), however, the new equilibrium is at E^1, the size of the multiplier being reduced by the rise in the price level. This analysis assumes that firms respond to the shift in the AD curve by raising real output because along the AS curve the money wage remains constant and if the price level increases real wages fall which results in an increase in real output and employment.

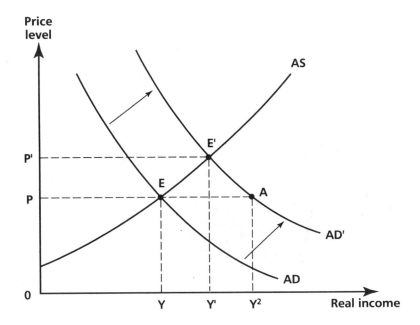

Figure 18.11

18 Short run and long run aggregate supply

With this method of analysis it is essential to consider more closely the characteristics of the AS curve. As a first step it is useful to distinguish between the **short run aggregate supply curve (SRAS)** and the **long run aggregate supply curve (LRAS)**.

Previously it was stated that the money wage remained constant along any particular AS curve and as a consequence any rise in the price level reduced real wages thus increasing real output along the curve. If however workers refuse to accept a reduction in real wages at this level of income and instead demand an increase in the money wage raising money wages in response to the rise in the price level, income and output cannot remain at Y^1 (Figure 18.11). In Figure 18.12 initial equilibrium is at point E^1 with price level P and output Y. Expansionary government policy then shifts the AD curve upwards to AD^1 with a new equilibrium at E^2 with output Y^1 and price level P^1. The rise in the price level reduces the real wage but the money wage is unchanged. With lower real wages firms increase employment and output. If however workers over time manage to raise their money wages, and hence their real wage also, the AS curve, which it will be recalled is associated with a constant money wage; shifts upwards to AS^1. As a consequence output and employment fall back to Y with equilibrium at E^3 and price level p^2, The money wage and price level have both risen in the same proportion which means that the real wage is back to its original level. Because firms now face the original real wage real output falls back to its original level but at a higher price level. Output is higher in nominal (value) terms but there is **no long run effect on real output, the only effect has been on the price level**. the long run as curve is therefore vertical, as indicated by the LRAS curve in Figure 18.12.

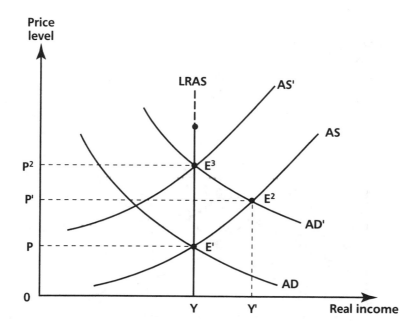

Figure 18.12

19 Adjustment lags

The time period over which the increase in real output can continue depends upon how quickly the money wage adjusts to the increase in prices. The length of this adjustment lag is closely associated with the role of expectations. In the rational expectations model expectations adjust instantaneously hence in the neo-classical model there is no distinction between the SRAS curve and the LRAS curve with no increase in output only the price level.

20 The wage-price spiral

The wage-price spiral discussed in Chapter 9 can also be illustrated by the use of AD and AS curves. The government may attempt to counteract the tendency for output and employment to return to its original level by giving a further boost to aggregate demand. In Figure 18.13 original equilibrium is at E with price level P and output Y, as in the analysis above AD is shifted to AD^1 raising output to Y^1 and the price level to P^1. Eventually however the money wage adjusts and the economy moves back as the AS curve shifts to AS$'$ on to the LRAS curve. As unemployment rises the government responds by boosting aggregate demand again and there is a move to a new equilibrium at E^3, but the economy again moves back to the LRAS curve with real output at Y and price level P^3. The succession of points such as E, E^1, E^2, E^3, E^4, represent the wage price spiral. At E^4 real output is the same as at E but with the price level at P^4. Output has risen only in nominal terms, unemployment is the same, but the price level (inflation) is much higher.

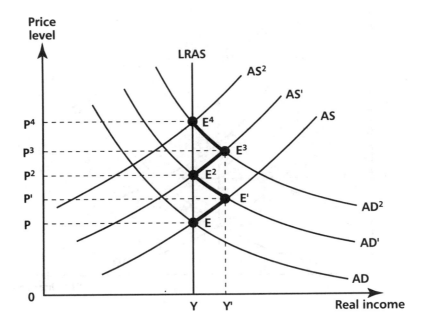

Figure 18.13

21 The Keynesian view

The Keynesian version of the AS curve is illustrated in Figure 18.14. In this version the AS curve is referred to as an L shape. Along the horizontal portion of the curve AD can be increased expanding output and employment with no conflict with the price level. When the full employment level of output is reached however any further increase in AD will lead to rising prices.

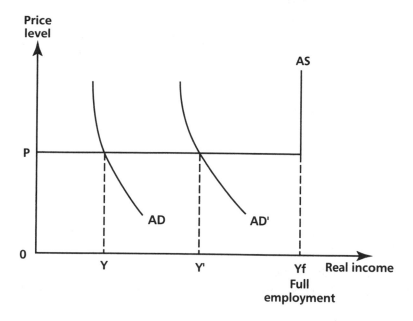

Figure 18.14

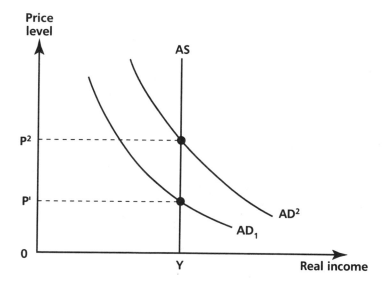

Figure 18.15

22 The neo-classical view

The extreme monetarist or neo-classical version is the vertical AS curve illustrated in Figure 18.15. In this version there is no scope for changes in AD to raise output, even in the short-run, the only affect of such policies will be to raise the price level, i.e. inflation.

23 Limitations

The implications of these models is crucially important as they indicate the limits to which governments are able to influence the economy through their policy measures. The superiority of any particular theory is however ultimately an empirical matter.

Self assessment questions

1 What does the IS curve represent?

2 What does the LM curve represent?

3 What is represented by the intersection of the IS and LM curves?

4 Explain the difference between the monetarist and Keynesian viewpoint by utilising IS-LM curves.

5 Under what circumstances would monetary policy be totally ineffective?

6 Explain the relationship between changes in money wage and shifts in the AS curve.

7 Distinguish between the Keynesian and neo-classical versions of the AS curve.

8 What is meant by supply side policies and why have they received more emphasis in recent years?

19

Economic growth and the UK economy

1 A definition

Economic growth refers to the increase in the economy's productive capacity. It is usual to express this in terms of the growth of gross domestic product (GDP).

Care must be taken in comparing GDP figures over time and making assumptions regarding economic growth from them for three reasons:

- Comparisons must take account of inflation and therefore can only be made in 'deflated' data, i.e. data at constant prices.
- An increase in GDP from a position of unemployed resources and deficient demand to one of full employment does not constitute economic growth as there has been no growth in productive potential. When comparisons between different time periods are made it is important therefore that the level of resource utilisation is similar.
- Even when GDP is growing, living standards may decline if the population growth is more rapid. Per capita GDP is the relevant measure and is calculated as:

$$\text{Per Capita GDP} = \frac{\text{GDP}}{\text{Population}}$$

2 The benefits of growth

Economic growth is generally considered to be desirable by governments because it enables them to achieve other policy goals which are considered desirable. Increased GDP implies higher incomes and therefore a higher standard of living in terms of material goods. Higher incomes also imply higher tax revenues for the government which should facilitate an improved level of provision of public services such as education, health, and other social services. The greater the rate of economic growth the more rapid the increase in living standards, as conventionally defined, will be.

3 British growth

The main cause of concern for the British economy has not been just the slow rate of growth which has been apparent but the fact that the growth rate has been slow relative to other industrial countries. Figure 19.1 indicates the UK's growth rate from 1967 to 1994 relative to other industrialised countries.

Britain's relatively poor performance is even more pronounced when the average figures over the period are considered. Japan averaged a growth in real per capita GDP of 4.3% per annum between 1967 and 1994, Germany 2.5% and the USA 2.4%. The UK over the same period averaged a growth in real per capita GDP of only 1.9%.

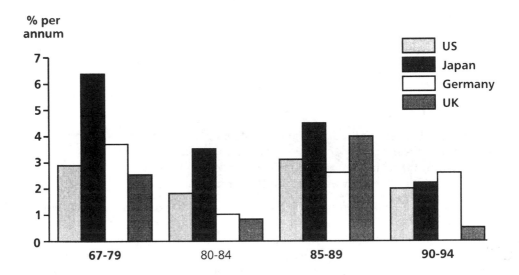

Figure 19.1

4 Sources of growth

In order to establish why growth rates differ it is necessary to identify the sources of economic growth. Economic growth is generated by an increase in both the **quality** and **quantity** of the nation's productive resources, in particular labour and capital.

● **Labour**
  – The **quantity** or **supply** of labour depends upon trends in the growth of working population, hours worked, the length of holidays and net migration.
  – The **quality** of labour is determined by the resources and facilities available for

training and education. Not only is the level of provision important but also the extent to which the skills being taught are appropriate to the needs of the economy as technological change takes place. The extent to which the labour force is willing to adapt to changes in technology and adopt new working practices is also an important factor. Investment in **human capital** has been identified as one of the major factors in generating economic growth.

- **Capital**
  - The size of the nation's stock of capital is an important factor in determining labour productivity. The more capital which is available per worker the greater will be labour productivity, referred to as the **capital:labour ratio**. The larger the proportion of GNP which a nation devotes to **investment** the greater will be the stock of capital. This **gross capital formation** is a major determinant of economic growth, however the precise stock of capital at any point in time is difficult to calculate due to the unreliability of the estimates of depreciation. Increasing the amount of capital per unit of labour is referred to as **capital deepening** whilst increasing the capital stock to keep abreast of increases in the size of the working population is referred to as **capital widening**. **Gross investment** refers to **new investment plus replacement investment** whilst **net investment** refers to **new investment** only. It is therefore possible to have gross investment without net investment.
  - The **quality** of the capital stock is of major importance, and in particular the extent to which it embodies the most recent technology, an element which is difficult to quantify but is of major importance in generating growth. The assumption is that the most recent machines incorporate the recent scientific and technical developments and are therefore more productive than older machines. This view suggests that gross investment is the most important figure even if most of it is replacement investment as this reduces the average age of the capital stock and therefore increases its quality and efficiency. The example of countries such as Germany and Japan is frequently quoted in support of this argument. These countries lost most of their productive capacity during the Second World War and replaced their capital stock with new equipment containing more recent technology which enabled them to make more rapid growth than countries such as Britain where the average age of the capital stock was much greater. This is sometimes referred to as the 'catching up' theory. Productivity gains due to improvements in the quality, rather than the quantity, of capital are said to result from **embodied technical change.**
  - **The incremental capital – output ratio (ICOR)** refers to the increase in output relative to the increase in capital (net investment) over a period. Figure 19.2 shows that the ICOR for the UK between 1964 and 1980 was considerably lower than in the other countries shown which suggests that regardless of the absolute proportion of GDP devoted to investment in the UK which was not significantly lower than the main trade competitors (see Figure 19.3), the quality of the investment decisions have not been particularly good. One reason suggested for this is that the tax system, through high rates of corporate taxation and investment allowance reduced the post tax rewards from investment whilst at the same time subsidising inefficient investment. Changes in the tax system since 1984 have been designed to introduce a more competitive climate for investment decisions by removing allowances and reducing the rate of corporation tax (see Chapter 7).

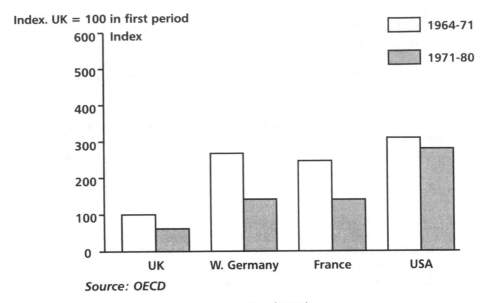

Source: OECD

Figure 19.2 Incremental capital – output ratios (ICOR)

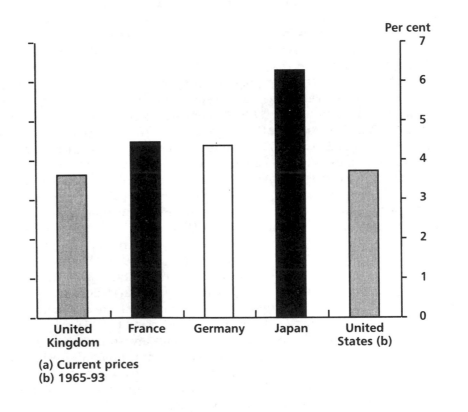

(a) Current prices
(b) 1965-93

Figure 19.3 Gross investment as a percentage of GDP

5 Production function

The importance for growth of not only increasing the amount of capital per worker (**capital deepening**) but also of incorporating the most recent technology (embodied technical change) can be illustrated by means of a simple **production function**. In this production function output (Q) is considered to be a function of capital (K), labour (L) and technological change (T)

i.e. $Q = T(t) f (K, L)$

Technological change is taken to depend only on time, and is neutral in that it affects the marginal productivity of both factors of production (K and L) equally. In Figure 19.4 the production function is plotted against output per worker, i.e. $q = \frac{Q}{L}$ and the capital/labour ratio, i.e. $K = \frac{K}{L}$ On production function PFN^0 technology is assumed to remain unchanged and the declining slope of the production function reflects the assumption of diminishing returns to increases in capital per worker. When the capital/labour ratio is increased from k^0 to k^1 output per worker increases from q^0 to q^1. However, when there is embodied technical change the production function shifts upwards to PFN^1, the new capital incorporating improved technology, as a consequence the same increase in the amount of capital per worker, k^0 to k^1 increases output per worker from q^0 to q^{11}, which is substantially greater. This analysis emphasises that the growth of output per worker depends upon two factors.

- Capital deepening as the capital/labour ratio increases.
- Embodied technical change capital – capital investment should incorporate the most recent technological advances.

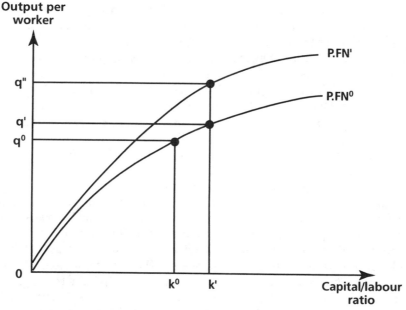

Figure 19.4

6 Technology; a source of economic growth

Denison[1] analysed the sources of economic growth in the United States over the period 1929–1969. The results of his analysis are shown in Table 19.1.

TABLE 19.1		
Total factor input		1.40
LABOUR	1.05	
CAPITAL	0.35	
Output per unit of input		1.82
Growth in national income		3.22

[1] Denison, E., 'Accounting for United States Economic Growth: 1929–69' (Brookings Institutions)

As shown in the table, national income grew at an **annual** rate of 3.22 per cent. Of this 3.22 per cent 1.40 per cent was attributable to the **growth of total factor inputs**, labour and capital and 1.82 per cent to the **growth of output per unit of factor input**. Of the growth due to increases in the **quantity** of factor inputs 1.05 per cent is attributed to the **growth of labour** input and 0.35 per cent to the **growth in capital.** Of the 1.05 per cent attributable to growth in labour input 0.49 per cent resulted from improvements in the educational attainments of the labour force. Growth in output per unit of input accounts for 1.82 per cent of growth, which is 57 per cent of total growth. Of this 1.82 per cent Denison attributes to advances in knowledge, i.e. **technological change. Economies of scale** resulting from increases in the scale of production accounted for 0.43 per cent of annual economic growth. These results illustrate the importance for economic growth of improvements in both the **quality** and **quantity** of factor inputs.

Changes in technology are the result of **research and development** and because technological change is so important for economic growth governments are generally keen to encourage high levels of research and development. They can do this either by undertaking research and development itself and making the results available to firms, or they may encourage firms to undertake it themselves by giving grants or other financial aid.

Technical change may apply to production techniques or to products. In both cases research and development are important, but in the case of new producers **market research** is also important. In the case of production techniques there are two important stages: **process innovation** which refers to the application by a firm of a new production technique, and **process diffusion** which is the application of the same technique by other firms. Product development also consists of two stages: product innovation which is the introduction of a new product by a firm, and product diffusion which is the introduction of similar new products by other firms. One criticism of UK firms, particularly in the field of micro electronics has been that they are technically very competent and achieve high levels of **invention** but fail to **innovate** new processes and products.

Firms introduce new technology into their production processes with the intention of reducing their costs. If reduction in costs is used merely in order to increase profitability by utilising more capital intensive production then the consequence will be a reduction in the amount of labour employed. However, if the firm uses its cost advantage to gain a larger market share and as a consequence greatly increases its output it may be able to maintain an unchanged labour force. The employment effects of new technology are one of the major issues facing society today.

The most significant technological change possibly in this century has been the advance in electronic **micro-technology** and in particular the advances in **micro computers**. The diffusion of this new technology into all areas of manufacturing and administration has been both extensive and rapid. It is now possible for large areas of production to be controlled by computers with them actually controlling the automatic tooling which performs the task, for example the use of robotics in motor car manufacture, referred to as computer aided manufacture (CAM). The use of computers has also spread significantly into the area of design with use of computer aided design (CAD). One area very significantly influenced by the application of micro computer technology is that of business administration. Many office functions are now performed by micro computers, for instance the storage and retrieval of information once performed by numerous clerks with filing cabinets can now be performed on a vast scale by a single operator with a micro computer. The routine typing of business letters can be performed by word processors as can the maintenance of routine accounting systems. The new technology has also influenced the way in which many businesses organise their management systems, for instance, in most firms the function of stock control, purchasing, production planning and distribution were treated as separate functions because of the sheer volume of information, which could only be handled by dividing it between specialised functions. Micro computers however provide the capacity to handle these vast amounts of data, and by utilising a common data base these functions are integrated into a single system, referred to as materials requirements planning (MRP). Newspaper publishing provides an example of the extent to which the nature of production in an industry can be changed by the advances in technology. Newspaper copy was originally written by the journalist who passed the copy to typesetters who set the typeface, the page layout also required careful design and finally the printing process employed large numbers of printers. Technology now enables the page to be printed directly from the journalist's copy, typed on a visual display unit, which can also be used to design the page layout. The printing machines are fully automatic and controlled by computer. As a consequence Express Newspapers were able to dispense with 5000 printing workers and move to a new plant employing only 500 journalists and electricians in the early 1980s.

Such changes clearly have profound employment implications. A permanently higher level of unemployment may be an inevitable consequence as technology takes over from labour. Many skills have become obsolete, increasing long term unemployment and creating the need for large scale retraining programmes. Semi-skilled employment has become scarcer as such tasks are generally easier to automate. Attitudes towards work may have to change, in particular towards the length of the working week, earlier retirement, the possibility of work sharing, and more part-time employment.

Some observers take a more optimistic view of employment prospects and suggest that although jobs will continue to be lost as a consequence of the new technology, many more will be created as new industries develop to take advantage of the technology, and with more leisure time there will be a growth in the leisure and service industries.

In future years it is unlikely that the majority of people will be able to pursue a career for life and attitudes towards career change may have to change. There is also the problem of income distribution, as the numbers displaced from work grow the income disparity between the employed and unemployed will grow unless the tax system is used for redistribution of income, in the form of unemployment benefit, for pensions, and to pay for education and retraining. Without income redistribution the ultimate question becomes – when all the goods are produced by robots, who will be able to buy them?

7 Other sources of economic growth

In the long run therefore it is the **supply of the factors of production** which determine economic growth. However, for the reasons stated above, the prospect of economic growth is attractive to governments and various measures have been adopted in the UK in the hope of achieving higher rates of growth. In planned economies it is less difficult to achieve a diversion of resources away from current consumption to investment and capital accumulation for future growth, but in a mixed economy with an electorate to appeal to resort has to be made to less direct means of stimulating growth. Measures which governments can utilise include:

- **Improvements in labour quality** by increasing the provision of education, and training of an appropriate type, in particular youth training.
- **Use of the tax system** in order to encourage investment, including allowances against tax for investment and depreciation. Differential rates of corporation tax on retained profits and dividends have also been used in the hope that lower rates on retentions would encourage a higher level of retentions and thereby increase investment (the extent to which such a policy is successful is however controversial).
- Keeping **interest rates low** and allowing tax relief on interest in order to reduce the cost of borrowing and improve the viability of investment projects.
- The encouragement of **research and development** by providing facilities and grants, and dispensing information from government sponsored research.
- Encouraging the acceptance of **new working practices** and **new technology** into industry by discussion with employer groups, trade unions and government sponsored bodies.
- The use of **public sector investment** as a source of growth. In particular capital spending on projects such as railway electrification and motorway construction.
- Maintaining a high level of domestic demand by the use of appropriate fiscal and monetary policy, although this may have costs in terms of inflation and the balance of payments which may in themselves damage long run growth prospects.

8 Government intervention

Governments have not however been particularly successful at improving growth rates. This is due largely to the problem of quantifying the relationship between the variables which are thought to influence growth and the amount of growth which changes in these variables actually generates. A further problem is that in a mixed economy too much intervention by government in order to achieve the growth objective may appear as a move towards central planning, hence the preference for indirect incentives. Britain's only attempt at planning for growth, in the form of the National Plan in 1965, attempted to stimulate growth by announcing a target growth rate of 4% per annum for 1964–1970, but was abandoned during its first year when an actual growth rate of only 2.4% was achieved. Failure was largely due to the problem discussed in Chapter 13 of achieving growth, balance of payments equilibrium, and price stability, simultaneously. During the period up to the early 1970s however, the main way in which governments in the UK attempted to achieve higher rates of growth was by maintaining a higher level of aggregate demand by pursuing expansionary fiscal policies in the Keynesian tradition of demand management.

The high rates of inflation experienced after the mid 1970s caused doubts to arise regarding the ability of governments to simultaneously control the level of inflation and maintain high levels of employment. The advent of the 'neo-classical' school of thought saw a fundamental questioning of the ability of governments to influence the growth of output and employment through demand management policies and placed more emphasis on the supply of the factors of production, both their quality and quantity, and more emphasis on the role of the free market.

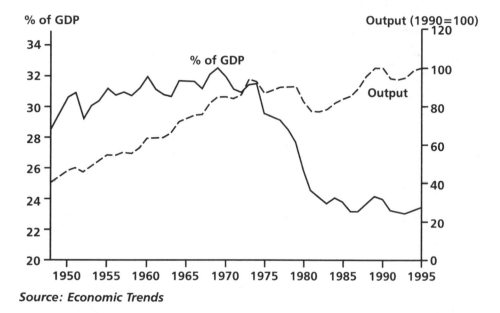

Source: Economic Trends

Figure 19.5

9 The decline in manufacturing

The report of the **House of Lords Select Committee on Overseas Trade** (HL 238,1985) associated Britain's low rate of growth with the **decline in the manufacturing sector.** Manufacturing output declined from 28 per cent of GDP in 1972 to 21 per cent in 1983, with the downward trend continuing. The trend of manufacturing output relative to GDP between 1950 and 1995 can be clearly seen in Figure 19.5. The decline in manufacturing output resulted in a reduction in manufactured exports which taken together with increased import penetration resulted in a deficit in the balance of trade in manufactures. This deficit on trade has however been compensated for in the balance of payments current account by the surplus on oil, with the advent of North Sea oil. The problem for the economy however will emerge when the North Sea oil reserves become depleted in the next decade and can no longer finance the trade deficit. The effect oil has had upon the balance of payments in the period 1985–95 can be seen from Figure 19.6(a) and (b): Figure 19.6(a) includes the export and import of oil whereas (b) shows only the situation with respect to oil.

The decline in the manufacturing sector of the UK economy has been accompanied by the growth of the service sector, over 60 per cent of GDP being derived from the service sector. The House of Lords report however suggested that sustained economic growth could not be based solely upon the service sector because it is itself totally dependent upon the growth of the manufacturing sector to use those services which it provides. Also, services are no substitute for manufacturers in overseas trade as only 20 per cent are tradable overseas. Sustainable growth therefore is only possible with a favourable trade balance in manufactures. Britain's balance of trade in manufactured goods over the period 1979–1995 is illustrated in Figure 19.7.

Balance on trade in goods 1985-95

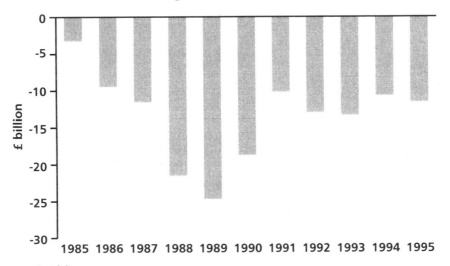

Figure 19.6(a)

The House of Lords Report identified the following reasons for the decline in manufacturing:

- The problem of being the **first industrial nation** developed on the basis of large overseas markets which have been eroded as other countries industrialised.
- **Lower rates of gross investment** than in competing countries. The reasons suggested for this included – lack of confidence placed by firms in the future, low profitability, high capital taxation, and high interest rates. Also other European countries and Japan needed to invest more rapidly than Britain after the Second World War in order to replace the capital assets which had been destroyed. Not only has investment been lower in the UK than in comparable countries but that investment has also been less effective in that the extra output from a given unit of additional capital has been lower, i.e. the incremental capital to output ratio (ICOR – see Figure 19.5). Reasons suggested

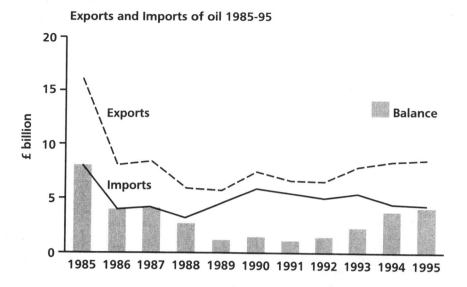

Figure 19.6(b)

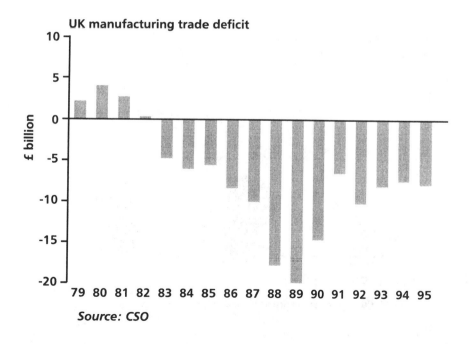

Source: CSO

Figure 19.7

for this included – insufficient emphasis on new products embodying new design and technology, too much investment in property and industries with lower productivity than manufacturing.

- **Cultural factors** were also identified as a reason for poor performance. Such factors, sometimes referred to as **X-inefficiency** lead to sub-optimal investment decisions and include; poor management, inadequate skills, and widespread resistance to change. Cultural factors extended to include a tendency to see manufacturing in an unfavourable light, to the extent that qualified people sought employment in other areas than manufacturing, associating success and achievement with other areas of employment.
- The **lack of investment** in earlier years has resulted in a situation where the **average age of Britain's capital stock is older than in most of our competitors'** and therefore incorporates less new technology. In order to compete prices have to be reduced which squeezes profits and in turn leads to even less investment. A vicious circle of uncompetitiveness and low growth.
- A number of **non-price factors** were also identified which affected the competitiveness of UK products in overseas markets. Some of these factors related to the product, such as; quality, reliability, suitability; and other factors were related to their marketing, such as; delivery times, after-sales service, sales representation, arrangements for marketing and quotations in inconvenient formats, e.g. Ex Works.
- **Poor price competitiveness** was identified as a major factor in Britain's poor overseas trade performance. Price competitiveness is influenced largely by factors such as poor labour productivity, wage rates, and the sterling exchange rate. UK competitiveness in manufacturing and overall is illustrated in Figure 19.8.

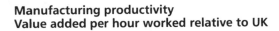

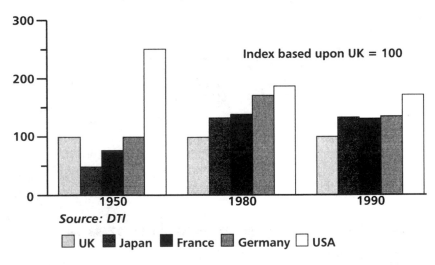

Figure 19.8

- The **high level of the sterling exchange rate**, particularly in the period after 1978 was seen as being a major factor in reducing UK price competitiveness. The rise in the exchange rate was attributed to two main factors, **North Sea oil** and **government policy**. The demand for North Sea oil kept the exchange rate at a higher level than would be justified by trade performance alone, hence it did not reflect underlying trends in the manufacturing sector. The government's medium term financial strategy kept **interest rates higher** than they would otherwise have been, resulting in capital inflows which put further upward pressure on the exchange rate. Government policy was also responsible for reducing domestic demand which had further exacerbated the decline in the manufacturing sector.

The report concluded that if Britain was to achieve success in manufactured trade, it would need a new sense of national purpose and improvements in all the areas of weakness outlined above. In particular the report called for a new national attitude towards manufacturing and trade, greater price and non price competitiveness, government macro-economic policies which favour manufacturing industry and are applied consistently, more government support for innovation and exports, more appropriate education and training, greater stability in the exchange rate, lower interest rates, a tax regime which favours manufacturing industry, improvements in both the quality and quantity of investment; and a greater inclination at all levels of society to purchase British manufactures. The process of 'de-industrialisation' is a major problem for the UK economy.

A further report appeared in 1994, the '1994 Competitiveness White Paper', as it became known, was the government's response to criticisms regarding their failure to address the issue of the manufacturing sector preferring to develop the financial sector. The white paper included schemes to deliver work related education, stimulate apprenticeships, help small and medium sized firms and reward imaginative manufacturing schemes.

The credibility of these proposals received a massive blow when in August of 1994 it was leaked that the government intended to axe some of the major parts of the DTI's aid to industry, especially the budget for regional selective assistance (RSA).

10 The drawbacks of growth

It is by no means universally accepted that economic growth is beneficial to society. Critics point to the following costs of economic growth:

- Deterioration of the environment through urban sprawl and industrialisation.
- The growth of environmental pollution to the atmosphere and rivers etc.
- High rates of innovation making skills redundant and forcing unwanted change or obsolescence onto people.
- The faster 'lifestyle' engendered by growth may bring in its wake illness and a reduced 'quality of life', e.g. heart attacks, ulcers, higher crime rates and suicide rates; which are all characteristic of urban industrialised societies.
- It may be argued that higher levels of consumerism are not necessarily synonymous with a better 'quality of life' and as quickly as 'wants' are satisfied then new wants can be created by the large corporations utilising skilful advertising. Constantly attempting to strive to new levels of 'satisfaction' can itself be a cause of stress in individuals, although it must be pointed out that most of the world's starving millions

would welcome the opportunity to enjoy at least some of the benefits of economic growth. Possibly the greatest challenge to economists in the remaining years of this century and into the 21st century will be how to achieve this growth in a responsible manner and ensure an acceptable distribution of its benefits.

11 UK growth

The slow growth rate exhibited by the UK economy in the post-war era saw a rapid improvement during the latter half of the 1980s, reaching a peak in 1988 of 4.7%. UK growth during this period compared favourably with the growth rates of the other industrial (G7) economies. The increase in growth was however accompanied by rising inflation, and a deterioration in the balance of payments as rising incomes and consumer spending caused imports to rise more rapidly than exports. 1990 however, saw the onset of recession as the rate of growth declined as a consequence of the government's counter-inflation policy of high interest rates, which restricted demand in the economy. The situation is illustrated in Figure 19.9. Despite some reductions in the rate of decline of GDP the UK economy stubbornly refused to exhibit signs of growth with the economy remaining stagnant well into 1993, despite government attempts to revive the economy through successive reductions in interest rates and the apparent evidence of 'green shoots'. Interest rates were reduced from a base rate of 15% in 1990 to 6% in January 1993, the lowest rate for 15 years with little, if any, effect on either the housing or consumer markets. Recent trends in interest rates are illustrated in Figure 19.10.

The problems of the UK economy were compounded by the decline of some of the other G7 economies in the period 1990–94, as can be seen in Table 19.2, making it even more difficult for the UK to achieve export led growth.

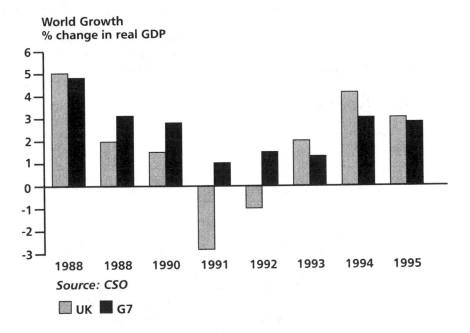

Source: CSO

Figure 19.9

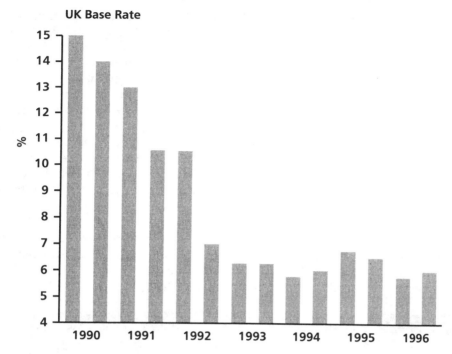

Figure 19.10

TABLE 19.2				
Growth of real GDP (%)				
	1967–79	1980–4	1985–9	1990–4
US	2.9	1.8	3.1	2.0
Japan	6.4	3.5	4.5	2.2
Germany	3.7	1.0	2.6	2.6
France	4.1	1.5	3.1	1.1
Italy	4.3	1.7	3.1	1.0
UK	2.5	0.8	4.0	0.5
EU	3.8	1.2	3.2	1.4

12 Inflation in the UK

Inflation has been a persistent problem for the UK, particularly as the rate of inflation has generally been higher than that of its trading partners making it more difficult to export to them. Following the 1988 peak in growth there was a substantial rise in inflation rates. This was due to the peak in growth and subsequent high growth rates being fuelled by a rapid increase in consumer spending. This 'consumer boom' was generated by a steady rise in real incomes, tax reductions in the March 1988 budget, a rapid rise in the money supply, as indicated in Table 19.3, and a decline in the savings ratio. Another contributory factor to the measured rate of inflation was the use of the interest rate as a counter inflation instrument. The rate of interest has a perverse effect in that it increases the cost of mortgages, which are included in the retail price index and therefore increases the rate of inflation. The 'underlying rate' of inflation is a measure of inflation which excludes mortgage interest payments (RPIX), and is considered to be a better measure for making international comparisons.

The rate of inflation rose to 10.9% in November 1990, however with the onset of recession the rate declined and by July 1993 stood at 1.2%, the lowest rate since 1964, whilst the underlying rate stood at 2.8%. The headline rate of inflation for July 1993 was lower than the European Union average of 3.3% and the G7 average of 2.7%. The fall in the rate of inflation during the period of recession was the result of reduced demand which lead to price cutting by business, and falling business costs. The reductions in the interest rates have resulted in an exaggerated fall in the RPI measure of inflation through the effect on mortgage payments, which have declined significantly. The underlying rate has fallen more slowly because, as stated earlier, they are excluded from this measure. Table 19.3 shows the rate of inflation in the UK over the period 1988 to 1996.

TABLE 19.3									
	1988	1989	1990	1991	1992	1993	1994	1995	1996
Money supply growth									
M4 /annual %) increase	15.0	18.5	18.2	12.0	5.4	2.9	6.0	4.85	10.0
Interest rates									
(Base rates)	13.0	15.0	14.0	10.5	7.0	6.2	5.8	6.6	5.75
Retail prices									
(Annual % increase)	4.9	7.8	9.5	5.9	3.8	1.6	2.5	3.4	2.8
Earnings per head									
(Annual % increase)	10.2	9.1	9.7	8.0	6.1	4.1	3.8	3.2	4.0

13 Savings behaviour

Experience of the 1960s and 1970s suggest that the growth of income is a significant influence upon savings behaviour. In 1969 the savings ratio (the ratio of personal savings to personal disposable income) was 8.1, this rose to 15.4 in 1980, before declining again as the rate of growth of incomes declined. By 1988 the savings ratio had declined to 5.

The reasons for the high level of the savings ratio in the 1970s and its decline in the 1980s are difficult to isolate. It is more convenient to consider the two periods separately.

- In the 1970s it is suggested that inflation was a major influence with the peaks in inflation and savings coinciding. One reason for this correlation is that inflation eroded the real purchasing power of the individual's liquid assets, and the level of savings was then increased in order to restore wealth to its previous level.

- The decline in the savings ratio, particularly in the latter half of the 1980s, is thought to be a consequence of the increased availability of credit and the more aggressive marketing of credit by financial institutions. A further influence may also be that the rise in property values increased the wealth of individuals to such an extent that they felt less need for savings and therefore increased their consumption. The reduction in the savings ratio together with the increased availability of credit were important elements in the UK consumer 'boom' of the late 1980s.

- The savings ratio rose from 5% in 1988 to around 11% in 1992. This increase may be attributed to a number of factors. One factor is the increased fear of unemployment, another is the high level of indebtedness incurred by consumers in the late 1980s, and also the reduction in wealth suffered by home owners due to the fall in property prices and the attempt by them to restore their net wealth to the previous levels. The increase in savings is a reflection of the lack of consumer confidence in the economy. The continued fear of unemployment and the failure of the property market to return to the boom of the early 1980s has continued to keep savings at a high level, despite low rates of interest, in the mid 1990s.

- Savings have been encouraged with the conversion of many building societies to banks and the incentives that have been on offer.

14 The 90s recession

The recession of the early 1990s is the longest since 1945 and the deepest for 60 years. This recession is also different from other recessions in a number of key aspects.

- The worst hit areas in terms of unemployment were the south-east of England, the south-west, and East Anglia rather than the traditional areas of the north of England, Scotland, Wales and Northern Ireland.

- The recession brought to an end the boom in house prices, particularly in the south-east of England. House prices in England declined between 1991 and 1993, and in the south-east, where the rise in prices had been greatest during the boom, prices declined by over 10%. Many home owners were left in a situation were they owed more on their mortgages than their property was worth, a situation referred to as **negative equity**. This not only makes it more difficult for people to move house causing stagnation in the housing market, but creates a reluctance to borrow which reduces consumption.

- The very high level of business failures, significantly higher than in earlier recessions, with 65,000 recorded failures during 1992.

15 Unemployment

Unemployment rose to a peak of 3.29 million in 1986 and then fell every month between 1986 and mid 1990, however the government's anti-inflation policy of high interest rates began to slow down the rate of growth and unemployment began to rise again. Between May 1990 and February 1993 the seasonally adjusted figure for unemployment rose from 1.66 million (5.8% of the workforce) to a peak of 2.96 million (10.6% of the workforce), after which it fell each month to a total of 1.93 million in November 1996.

The largest impact of unemployment, as in the two most recent earlier recessions, fell on the manufacturing sector. Recent trends in unemployment are illustrated in Figure 19.11 below.

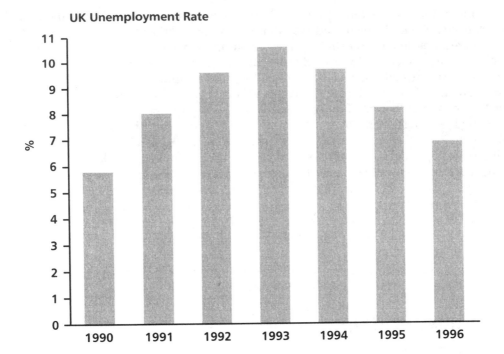

UK Unemployment Rate

Figure 19.11

16 PSBR/PSDR

During the second half of the 1980s the government was successful in its objective of reducing the ratio of public expenditure to GDP This achievement was partly due to the reduction in unemployment and the subsequent reduction in social security spending. The ratio of general government expenditure (GGE) to GDP stood at 39.5% by 1990. The government's success in reducing the percentage of GGE enabled it, by 1987, to convert the public sector borrowing requirement (PSBR) into the public sector debt repayment (PSDR) i.e. from budget deficit to budget surplus. During 1991 however a PSBR re-emerged growing rapidly to a massive £45 billion for 1993/94 which is approximately 7% of GDP, with GGE rising to 45% of GDP. Recent trends in the PSBR are illustrated in Figure 19.12. This growth in the PSBR is a consequence of the deepening recession which resulted in increased government expenditure on social security benefits whilst government receipts from taxation fell. How to fund this PSBR without damaging the potential for growth in the economy is a major problem for government economic policy.

17 The balance of payments

The rapid growth in consumer demand between 1986 and 1989 resulted in a widening of the current account deficit to £8 billion with a deficit of £14 billion on the non-oil account. The deterioration in the balance of payments continued during 1989 and the deficit for 1989 stood at £20.3 billion, the highest ever recorded, amounting to 4.5% of GDP. This was mainly due to the deterioration in visible trade as imports rose more rapidly than exports. Consumer demand slowed down during 1990 reducing the size of the deficit, however as the recession deepened instead of the balance of payments improving as may normally be expected, after 1991 the deficit grew to £11.2 billion for 1993. The improvement shown in 1994 was again reversed in 1995 with a deficit of £6.0 billion. Britain's trade position reflects the underlying weakness of the manufacturing sector but in recent years the trade in invisibles has also weakened. Figure 19.13 illustrates recent trends in the current account deficit.

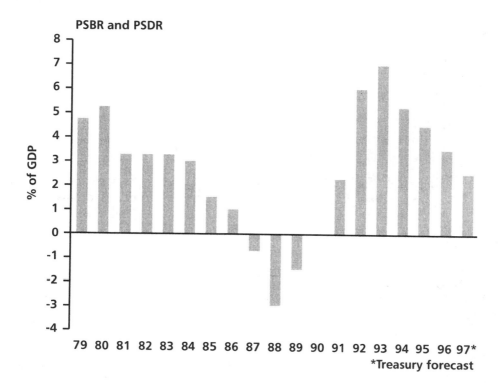

Figure 19.12

The fall in the value of sterling following Britain's withdrawal from the European Exchange Rate Mechanism (the ERM) should have made British exports more competitive but it is doubtful whether British industry was strong enough to take advantage of this.

Following the decline in sterling during 1986 and increases in productivity which reduced per unit labour costs manufacturing output increased significantly. These productivity gains substantially improved the profitability of UK companies and made a genuine contribution to the improved growth rate of that period.

With the onset of recession in 1991 output and therefore profits fell; however, profit margins stood up to recession surprisingly well. This is due to the ability to constrain cost, particularly labour costs, and substantial improvements in labour productivity. This rise in productivity can be clearly seen in Figure 19.14

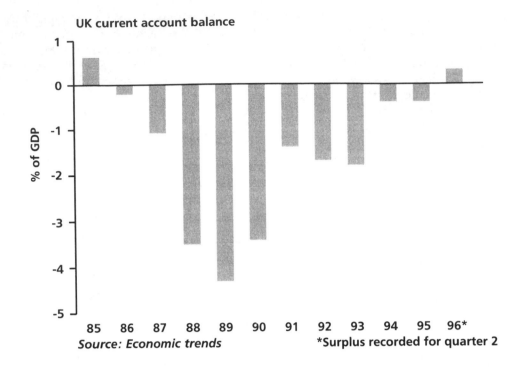

Figure 19.13

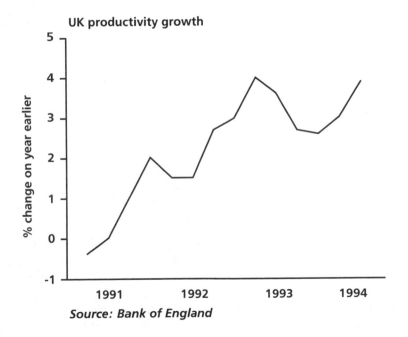

Figure 19.14

18 Interest rate movements

The government's response to the growth in consumer demand and the subsequent rise in inflation and deterioration in the balance of payments was to attempt to reduce the growth in demand by increasing interest rates. The economy however was slow to respond to higher interest rates subsequently requiring further increases. Interest rates were increased from 9 to 15% in eleven successive increases during the second half of 1988 and 1989. Interest rate increases however affect investment demand as well as consumer demand and by the final quarter of 1990 the UK economy entered recession. The depth of the recession was made worse by Britain's membership of the ERM. Sterling was over-valued against the other member currencies making exports dearer and imports cheaper, and the need to maintain the value of sterling within the mechanism forced the government to keep interest rates at an artificially high level, up to 15% just prior to leaving the ERM.

Following Britain's withdrawal from the ERM the value of sterling fell against other major currencies and the government was able to reduce interest rates to 6%. Interest rates have remained below 7% with only mild fluctuations. This has resulted in a steady increase in growth and a rise in employment. Retail sales began to pick up towards the end of 1995 whilst the underlying inflation rate (RPIX) has remained within 0.3% of the target rate of 2.5%. The growth in manufacturing has been quite marked towards the end of 1996 leading to an improved export performance.

It has been suggested that the 'feelgood' factor has returned. The weak recovery that began in 1992 has begun to translate itself into better living standards. However the upward pressure on consumer spending in the first half of 1997 caused fears of an increase in the rate of inflation, consequently the Bank of England exercised its new independence over interest rate policy and raised interest rates three times in succession to a base rate of 6.75% in July 1997, the highest rate in the G7 economies. The higher level of interest rates resulted in an appreciation in the value of sterling against other major currencies in the order of 25%. This in itself could have a deflationary impact upon the UK economy, but may also have an impact upon export performance.

Self assessment questions

1 Account for the relatively poor performance of the UK economy in the post-war era.

2 Although economic growth is generally considered desirable, what are its disadvantages?

3 Identify the main sources of economic growth.

4 Summarise the main trends in the UK economy between 1985 and 1995.

20
Development economics

1 The development gap

Although in the advanced economies of the Western world economic growth for its own sake has been the subject of criticism, for many areas of the world the achievement of economic growth is of overriding concern as it is seen as the means by which the less developed countries can raise the living standards of their populations. Only about 20% of the world's population enjoy a standard of living comparable to that of Western Europe, and over half of the world's population live in extreme poverty, in fact the United Nations (UN) definition of under-developed economies place most of the world's population in the category of 'the underdeveloped South'. In many of the poorest countries, where the growth rates are lowest, the gap between these and the wealthier Western economies becomes even wider.

2 Characteristics of under-developed countries

These under-developed countries of the South or 'Third World' countries are not sufficiently developed to generate the necessary domestic savings required to finance the investment necessary for industrialisation and subsequent economic growth. Current income is barely adequate for current consumption. These countries are characterised by some, or all of the following:

- Rapid population growth.
- Low per capita income.
- Low levels of per capita investment.
- A low volume of investment in 'social' capital and infrastructure, i.e. roads, railways, schools, hospitals etc.
- A tendency to rely on the production of a narrow range of agricultural commodities whose prices are low, and subject to wide and rapid fluctuations on world markets. As a result incomes are low and variable. An example is the concentration on coffee production in Central America.

3 The advantages of growth

The obvious questions which those in the developed countries may ask regarding the under-developed economies are; firstly, why should we be concerned, and secondly; why is economic growth seen as being the solution to the problems of the 'Third World' countries?

- Any civilised society must feel some moral obligation to those fellow human beings living in abject poverty and often suffering mass starvation. This feeling has been clearly demonstrated by the generosity shown by millions of people in the 1985 Live Aid appeal, to help those dying of famine in Ethiopia. Such emergency aid can of course not solve the underlying problems of these countries but does demonstrate the willingness of people to help when they are made aware of the problem.
- Economic growth is seen as being a desirable objective for under-developed countries because it should eventually enable them to support their growing populations by producing sufficient commodities, goods and services to enable them to engage in international trade and thereby earn the necessary foreign currency which would enable them to raise the living standards of their people by paying for the import of the goods they cannot produce themselves.
- Ignoring the humanitarian arguments there are distinct economic advantages for the Western World in the improvement of the economies of third world countries. Firstly if these countries could improve their performance in the production of those goods in which they have a comparative advantage and the developed countries could increase their trade with them, then according to the law of comparative advantage, greater specialisation could take place, which would raise world output to the material advantage of all concerned. Secondly if these economies can develop they will provide an enormous new market for the output of the developed economies of the West. The people of the third world countries are potential consumers as well as producers and the future prosperity of the West may depend upon the development of these new export markets.
- Many of the under-developed countries have suffered in the past from political instability, a feature which has not been helped by various governments using the patronage of aid to exert political influence. The achievement of an adequate growth rate however should enable a country to be independent of the influence of other governments and develop its own political institutions.

4 Barriers to growth

If the problems of the under-developed countries are to be overcome it is necessary to identify clearly the **barriers to growth** which exist. These barriers to growth are as follows:

- **Population growth** is a major factor limiting economic development. The rapid growth in population means that even if the economy is growing in terms of national income, if population growth is faster than the growth of national income then per capita incomes will be falling. The sort of situation described by Thomas Malthus in the 18th century. In fact some of the poorest countries suffer from both a low growth rate and a high growth rate of population. The expression 'critical minimum effort' is used to refer to an increase in national income which is sufficiently large to provide an increase in per capita living standards despite the increase in population and is a critical stage in the generation of sustained growth.

- **Limitations to resource use**: even where countries have natural resources they may not be able to utilise them effectively. The limits to efficient resource utilisation result from a variety of factors but include shortages of financial capital, lack of 'social' overhead capital (inadequate infrastructure), deficiencies in human capital, and climatic difficulties. It should be noted, however, that material resources are not an essential requirement for economic development, for example the so-called 'tiger' economics of Taiwan, Singapore, Hong-Kong, and Korea whose rapid growth in manufacturing output has been based upon a hard working labour force, low wages, innovativeness and overseas investment.

- **Human capital deficiencies** can be a further brake on development. Even though the population is growing rapidly there may be severe shortages of skills and educated personnel. Also, many of the labour force may suffer from debilitating diseases such as bilhazia, malaria, and cholera, which reduce productivity. A further problem is that these countries may have no entrepreneurial class who are trained and motivated to organise resources efficiently for production, which was a particular feature of ex-colonial countries where local people were denied the opportunities to develop such skills.

- **Inefficient use of resources** is a further problem distinct from shortages of resources. These inefficiencies derive from two sources:
  - **Allocative inefficiency** i.e. investment of society's resources in making the wrong products.
  - **'X' inefficiency** results where investment is in the right product but is not being used as efficiently as is possible i.e. is suboptimal. This results from inadequate education and training, poor health, lack of motivation, religion, customs and taboos. This has been identified as a major cause of low growth in many underdeveloped countries and there are large economic benefits to be gained from overcoming it.

- **Capital accumulation** is an essential pre-requisite of economic growth; however capital accumulation requires that some current consumption be foregone. This becomes virtually impossible where living standards are already at a level where survival is difficult. For this reason developing countries have been forced to rely upon borrowed capital. The problem with this form of capital accumulation is the future debt burden it generates which consists of both the debt and the accumulated interest. Ironically such was the scale of lending to third-world countries in the 1970s that by 1984 debt repayment constituted a net transfer from those countries to the developed nations as it outweighed the sum of aid and new lending. In the past a further problem was that loans were tied to specific projects which proved to be inappropriate, for example prestige investments which required a level of technological sophistication which was beyond the capability of the recipient nation (elaborate hydro-electric generation schemes with no distribution system, for example).

5 The free market versus aid

There are two approaches which have been advocated for solving the problems of the developing countries, a free market 'trade' approach and a planned 'aid' approach, sometimes referred to as the 'trade versus aid' argument.

- The 'planned aid' approach is criticised by those who favour a free market 'trade' approach on the following grounds:

- Investment decisions made by government civil servants may not be made upon sound commercial criteria but rather opting for more prestigious projects with a lower return.
- There is no guarantee that the aid will ever reach the poor for whom it was intended and may instead be used by an inefficient, uncaring and non-representative government to retain power for itself and to enhance the personal prestige of those involved.
- Aid is demeaning to the recipient and by removing the incentives to work and innovate reduces the capacity of a people for self help. The recipient country is put into the position of being a beggar which is both demoralising and undignified.
- After many years of aid it has made very little impact on the problems of the recipient nations.
- During periods of recession in the donor countries aid may result in a feeling of resentment towards the recipients.

- Proponents of the free market, or trade, approach place great emphasis on human inventiveness, initiative and effort. They suggest that once the economy has a sound infrastructure entrepreneurs responding to market prices will develop the economy far more rapidly than any planning body composed of civil servants. The free market approach emphasises the giving of commercial loans in preference to aid and the reduction of tariffs and other barriers in order to encourage trade. Supporters of the trade solution to the problem emphasise the following points:
  - Commercial loans will be used for investment in industries which show the highest rates of return, hence resource utilisation will be more efficient. Industries with the highest rates of return will generally be those which offer the greatest potential for generating economic growth.
  - Increased trade will encourage specialisation according to the laws of comparative advantage which will result in a growth in total world output.
  - The market solution relies on people's own efforts and initiatives and is more dignified than aid.

- When criticising aid it must be borne in mind that timely aid has sometimes saved millions of lives, for example during the Ethiopian famine of 1984. However just handing out food in such situations only deals with the symptoms rather than overcoming the problem. If, for example, deliveries of grain cannot be distributed to those in need then the whole effort is wasted. Hence the tendency in modern aid programmes is to spend aid money on vehicles and low technology irrigation schemes, for example, as well as on food provision for the immediate problem.

Regarding the free market solution it must be remembered that the present development gap is a result of 200 years of the operation of market forces and trade, where the benefits go to those who are strongest in the market place and the relative strength in the market is determined by the initial starting points of those involved. The market solution does not indicate how this development gap can be narrowed. It may be that a planned aid programme can be used to raise economic development to a point where the developing economy can be exposed to the rigours of world trade in order to generate further growth. Some of the Newly Industrialised Countries (NICs) of Asia such as India, China, and the 'Tiger' economies mentioned earlier, may be considered in this category.

The post-war era has seen the implementation of both approaches to the development problem with the development of various agencies for both the implementation of aid schemes and for the encouragement of trade with the developing countries.

6 Aid agencies

It would be impossible to give here full details of all the agencies involved with aid in the post-war period hence a brief outline of the major developments only will be given, but this should be sufficient for most purposes.

- The **International Monetary Fund (IMF)** was established by the Bretton Woods agreement of 1944, effective from 1947; to administer the Fixed Exchange Rate system. As part of the system a fund was created to assist member countries with temporary - balance of payments difficulties. In order to increase international credit a system of Special Drawing Rights (SDR's) were later introduced, these SDR's were distributed amongst member countries according to their fund quotas and could be included in their official reserves and therefore form a basis for payment, thereby increasing international liquidity.

- The **International Bank for Reconstruction and Development (IBRD)** was also established at the Bretton Woods Conference in 1944 and became effective from 1946. The purpose of the bank is to encourage capital investment for the reconstruction and development of its member countries either by channelling the necessary private funds or by making loans from its own resources. It also makes loans to ease the balance of payments problems of the developing countries, these loans may be conditional upon the recipient country's adopting economic policies specified by the bank. The IBRD through its affiliated institution, the International Development Association (IDA), also gives long term loans at low or zero interest for projects in the developing countries, the loans are intended mainly for infrastructure investment such as roads or power supply. The repayment period for such loans may be up to 50 years.

- The **United Nations Conference on Trade and Development (UNCTAD)** was convened in 1964 in response to growing anxiety amongst the developing countries over their difficulties in closing the development gap. Since then UNCTAD has convened 5 times in total in order to promote Third World interests. UNCTAD 5 met in 1979 at Arusha, Tanzania, and emphasised a need for collective self reliance through North-South co-operation.

- The **Brandt report** (officially entitled North-South; A Programme for Survival) was published in 1980. The report emphasised the dangers inherent in the growing gap between the rich countries of the north and the poor countries of the south. The report was very wide in its scope but included the following proposals:
  - Increased aid to the south rising to 1% of GNP of the wealthier countries by the year 2000.
  - Increased international liquidity for the south through the issue of Special Drawing Rights (SDR's) by the IMF.
  - The stabilisation of Third World commodity prices at remunerative levels and the loosening of the wealthy nations grip on processing and marketing.
  - Doubling of the lending by the IBRD.
  - The removal of tariffs and other barriers to trade with Third World Countries.
  - The creation of a World Development Fund financed automatically by international taxes on trade, arms sales and sea bed exploration.
  - Regarding debt the report stated that assistance should be given to the South to enable them to maintain the interest payments on their debts and that more debts should be written off . It was also suggested that more loans should be given rather than grants and that these loans should not be tied to specific projects.

The Brandt report covered many other areas such as agrarian reform and the prolifera-
tion of nuclear weapons. Little progress was made on the points included in the report
however as fear of inflation and unemployment in the North during the 1980s meant that
governments, in particular the US, who were cutting their own public expenditure budgets, were unwilling to fully support such measures.

7 Britain's growth and aid

As Britain's growth rate improved during the latter part of the 1980s the proportion of
GDP devoted to aid actually declined from 0.52% in 1979 to 0.28% in 1987. This further
declined in 1996 to 0.31%. The major financial problem to emerge for the developing
countries has been that of meeting the interest repayments on their debts.

8 The debt problem

During the latter half of the 1980s the debt problem of the less developed countries
remained at the forefront of international discussion. The two main groups of countries
which have faced serious problems in servicing their debt are the 15 middle income
debtors, and the much poorer countries of sub-Saharan Africa.

The present top ten debtor countries are shown in Figure 20.1

Although a large number of countries have had to reschedule their debts since 1982, a
substantial majority of the population of the developing world lives in countries which
have had no major problems in meeting their debt obligations.

Much of the debt accumulated during the 1970s when the external environment was
highly favourable to international borrowing, real interest rates were often negative and
the prices of primary commodities were rising. Unfortunately much of this bank finance
was not well used. Some of it was wasted, some of it left the borrowing country again
('capital flight') and some of it was invested in uneconomic projects or in sectors with no
comparative advantage in trade, or was used merely to finance current consumption.
Usually the capital borrowed failed to produce sufficient income to pay the interest on
the loans. As a consequence the burden of the debt accumulated and resulted in a worsening of those countries' economic position.

9 The debt burden

The problem was accentuated in the 1980s as the world environment became much less
favourable. Growth in export markets had slowed down. Also the real burden of debt
rose very sharply with the rise in real interest rates, as nominal rates fell more slowly than
the rate of inflation in creditor countries. In addition the prices of commodities fell
sharply on world markets.

10 The banks and third world debt

The extent of loans from banks in the UK and USA by 1982 totalled more than the banks'
entire capital base and concern began to focus on the risk this presented to the entire
banking system as the debtor countries found it increasingly difficult to meet their debt
repayments.

Top ten debtor countries in 1992	
	($ million)
Brazil	121.3
Mexico	113.4
Indonesia	84.4
Russian Federation	78.7
India	76.9
China	69.3
Argentina	67.6
Turkey	54.8
Poland	48.5
Republic of Korea	43.0

Figure 20.1
Source: World Bank, 1994

After 1982, the banks that lent to problem debtors reinforced their balance sheets. In particular they increased their capital in relation to their exposure to these debtors. Between 1982 and 1986 banks managed to reduce loans to problem debtors as a proportion of their total assets. In the UK this percentage declined from 9.3% to 6.9% and in the US from 6.8% to 5.4%. They also increased their capital as a proportion of problem loans, from below 100% in both cases to about 130% for US banks and 140% for UK banks.

Some countries, such as Peru and Zambia, placed limits on their debt service payments and others, like Brazil, did not pay interest due. Some debts were traded on the market at less than their face value, reflecting the market's view that they might not be fully repaid or serviced.

Commercial banks took other steps, in addition to increasing their capital, to improve their provisions against the risk of bad debts. The National Westminster Bank announced it would increase provisions by about £0.5 billion, and the Midland Bank did likewise by just under £1 billion. Two of the largest banks in the US announced that they were making provisions totalling $4.7 billion and others followed. The US and UK governments welcomed these moves.

11 Banks' response to debt

Stronger balance sheets mean that banks are now better able to decide on new lending to debtor countries on normal commercial criteria, rather than as a means of ensuring that interest payments from debtors remain current and to maintain the value of existing exposure. Some banks have been reluctant to contribute their share to new lending packages and these have become increasingly difficult to put together.

In the next stage some banks may wish to limit their exposure by buying their way out of participation in future concerted lending. This could be achieved by purchasing securities such es 'exit bonds'. Better provisioning will also open up opportunities for banks to participate in other ways, such as interest capitalisation, or debt for equity swaps. This more market-orientated 'menu approach' may replace the concerted lending packages that have been the norm since 1982.

12 Debt/export ratios

While the banks have strengthened their position, that of problem debtors has not on average improved. Although the interest burden on their outstanding debts has fallen slightly as a proportion of export earnings since 1982, the actual amount of debt outstanding has risen in relation to the size of their economies.

Despite the progress that has been made to date, the external position of many debtors, particularly the poorer countries in sub-Saharan Africa, is worse now than it was in 1982. Debt/export ratios are higher; the valuation of debt in secondary markets has fallen; capital flight has continued; and there has been little or no help from spontaneous financial inflows. In many cases reform programmes have not been maintained consistently. But some debtors, especially outside Africa and Latin America, have continued to service their debts on schedule.

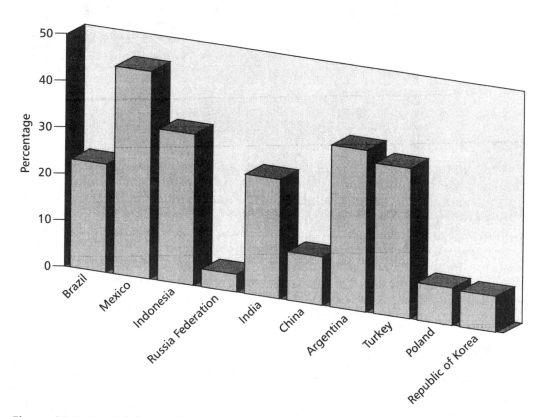

Figure 20.2 Total debt service as % of exports of goods and services
Source: World Bank 1994

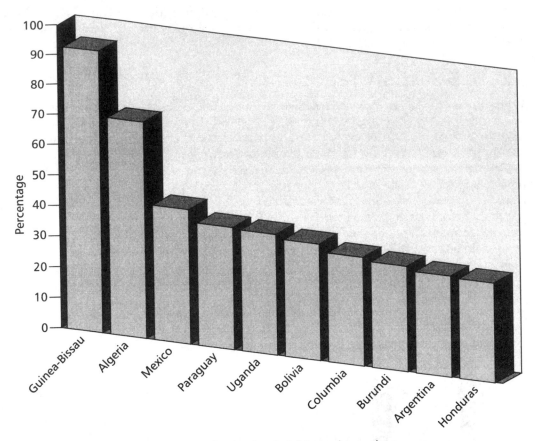

Figure 20.3 Top ten debtors on the basis of debt service ratio
Source: World Bank 1994

13 Recent debt management

The main method of helping the debtor countries has been through the provision of additional finance and domestic economic reform but the poorest countries of sub-Saharan Africa also need to have some of their debt burden removed. The middle income debtors in Latin America and elsewhere have the resources to put themselves on the road to recovery whilst the poorest countries do not. Also middle income debt is owed mainly to commercial banks, and so is primarily for debtor countries and banks to manage. In the poor countries, however, the debt is mainly owed to official investors who must consequently be involved in helping the countries concerned to find a solution.

14 The Paris Club

Assistance for the poorest countries, generally those of subSaharan Africa, has been through the re-scheduling of loans. The rescheduling of debts owed to governments is generally conducted by the Paris Club. The Paris Club renegotiates the terms of debts owed to government creditors whilst debts owed to commercial banks are dealt with separately by the banks and debtors themselves. The Club first met in 1956 and membership consists of creditors, usually the major industrial countries, who wish to be represented at discussions regarding particular debtors. Since 1956 the Club has carried out 130 re-schedulings for 46 countries, covering over $90 billion of outstanding debt, the majority since the emergence of the debt problem in the early 1980s.

15 Toronto Summit

In April 1987 at a summit meeting in Toronto the UK launched its initiative on sub-Saharan debt. The initiative was agreed at a meeting of the Paris Club in August 1988 with the final details settled by the finance ministers of the G7 countries in Berlin in September 1988. Under the agreement very poor and 'debtdistressed' countries who were pursuing sound economic adjustment programmes, approved by the IMF, should receive concessional terms when their debt was re-scheduled. Following the new agreement, creditors would choose from a 'menu' of three options when re-scheduling debt. The three options are:

- Reducing the interest charged on the re-scheduled debt by 3.5 percentage points (or halving it, if that is less than three percentage points).
- Writing off one third of the total volume of the debt.
- Re-scheduling the debt over a very long period (25 years compared with the normal 10).

The first option is the one which the UK will normally adopt.

16 Recent experience

By 1989 the burden of debt was leading to political instability in several countries, in particular Venezuela where rioting due to food shortages and price rises resulted in many deaths. This led to the announcements in March 1989 of an initiative by the United States to reduce the level of debt. The proposal was that the US was prepared to waive banking regulations to encourage commercial banks to reduce debts and to use its strong voting power at the World Bank and the IMF to provide fresh funds to reduce both the principal and interest payments by Third World Countries. This resulted in an increase in international bank lending in 1992, as well as private flows, followed by a low point in 1993 for both sources of finance.

The crisis in Mexico in 1994, created by political instability and economic uncertainty, resulted in yet another attempt by the USA and the IMF to produce a rescue package that would aid not only Mexico but all of the developing countries. In 1993 developing countries' external debt stood at $1630 bn.

17 Some conclusions

The problem of the developing nations is the greatest challenge to economies but may in the long run offer the greatest prospect for growth in world output and living standards.

Self assessment questions

1 What are the barriers to growth in the under-developed countries?

2 Distinguish between the trade and aid approaches to assisting the under-developed countries.

3 Why does debt repayment create such a burden for the underdeveloped countries?

4 What is meant by the 're-scheduling of debt'?

Glossary of economic terms

Accelerator Coefficient. The amount of additional capital required to produce a unit increase in output in the accelerator model.

Accelerator – Multiplier Model. A model which explains the fluctuations in the trade-cycle through the interaction of the accelerator principle and the multiplier.

Accelerator Principle (The). A capital stock adjustment process which proposes that the level of investment varies directly with the level of income (output).

Ad Valorem Tax. Indirect taxes which are a 'proportion of value'.

Advanced Countries. Industrially advanced countries with the highest levels of national income per head.

Aggregate Monetary Demand (AMD). The total demand for goods and services in the economy. Assumed to consist of the demand for consumption goods (C), plus investment goods (I) by firms, plus the demand by government (G), plus the demand for exports (X) minus imports (M). As aggregate demand determines the level of output (income) it also determines the level of employment. It is central to the Keynesian model of demand management. Therefore AMD = C+l+G+(X–M).

Aggregate Supply. The total supply of all goods and services available from domestic production plus imports to meet aggregate demand.

Arbitrage. The practice of buying in one market at a low price and reselling in another market at a higher price. Eventually the practice will eliminate the price difference between the two markets. May occur with the switching of short term funds between financial markets with different interest rates or exchange rates.

Asymmetric Information. A cause of market failure where some economic agents have more knowledge or information than others. The parties do not have equal bargaining power. In the theory of the firm it is seen in the separation of ownership from control in that managers have more information than shareholders.

Autonomous Investment. That proportion of total investment not determined by economic factors, such as the rate of interest, but by factors such as technical innovation.

Average (Total) Cost. The total cost of production divided by output to give the average cost of production per unit.

Average Propensity to Consume (APC). The proportion of national or individual income which is used for consumption purposes.

Average Propensity to Save (APS). The proportion of national or individual income which is saved, i.e. not used for consumption. It is the complement of the APC and therefore measured as 1–APC.

Balance of Payments. An account summarising the UK's transactions with the rest of the world. Divided into two sections: the current account and the capital account. The current account is composed of visible trade (goods) and invisible trade (services). The capital account consists of flows of funds for investment purposes and loans. There may be a surplus or deficit on the current account.

Balanced Budget. Refers to the budget of the central government which is said to balance when the receipts from taxation are sufficient to meet the government's expenditure. Since 1945 UK budgets have generally been in deficit.

Balanced Budget Multiplier. The proposition that even when an increase in government expenditure is exactly matched by an increase in taxation it is still possible to have a multiplier effect on national income

Bank of England. The central bank of the UK. Established in 1694 and nationalised in 1946 and given independence in 1997. It is responsible for implementing the government's monetary policy and acting as banker to the government. It is also responsible for the issue of bank notes and coins through the issuing department.

Barriers to entry. Characteristics of a market, either economic or technical, designed to raise the costs of firms wishing to enter that market and so deter them from entering.

Beveridge Report. Prepared by Lord Beveridge in 1942 on social insurance and allied services at the request of the government. It contained a plan for social security based on three aspects; a health service, child allowances, and full employment.

Birth Rate (Crude). The average number of live births occurring in any year for every 1000 of the population.

Black Economy. That part of a country's economic activity which is not officially recorded as part of the national income. Referred to as 'black' as it is untaxed. Currently about 10% of gross domestic product in the UK.

Brandt Report. The report of the commission of inquiry into the problems of the developing countries under the chairmanship of Herr Willy Brandt. Published in 1980 entitled 'North-South: A Programme for Survival'.

Bretton Woods Conference. Bretton Woods, New Hampshire 1944, a conference to consider proposals for the settlement of post-war payments problems. Resulted in the system of fixed exchange rates, the IMF and the IBRD.

Budget Deficit. Occurs when the central government's expenditure exceeds revenue from taxation, the deficit covered by borrowing. Advocated by Keynes (J.M.) as part of the process of demand management. The normal situation in the UK in the post-war period.

Budget Surplus. When central government revenue exceeds expenditure. In the UK a surplus, established 1987, is referred to as public sector debt repayment (PSDR).

Built-In (Automatic) Stabilisers. Features in a modern tax and benefit system which tend to automatically dampen down fluctuations in income and employment. For example, as incomes rise recipients move into higher taxation brackets which dampens down inflationary tendencies. As unemployment rises the increase in welfare benefits automatically increases, maintaining the level of aggregate demand.

Capital. The stock of physical assets utilised in the act of production which are themselves the result of production. Generally taken in economics to be buildings, plant and machinery, i.e. physical goods or real capital.

Capital Expenditure. The purchase of fixed assets such as plant and equipment.

Capital Formation. Net (new) investment in fixed assets, i.e. additions to the stock of capital.

Cartel. A group of firms within an industry who collude to regulate prices and/or output in their own interests, thereby reducing or eliminating competition .

Central Bank. A feature of all developed economies, it is the instrument by which governments implement monetary policy and control banking and credit creation. In the UK also a bankers' bank and 'lender of last resort' to the discount market.

Clearing Banks. Banks which utilise the London bankers clearing house for the settlement of claims among themselves. Generally taken to be the same as the commercial banks.

Closed Economy. A simplifying device for purposes of national income analysis by which an economy is assumed to have no imports and no exports, i.e. no foreign trade.

Cobweb Theorem. A model in which the quantity currently supplied depends upon the price which prevailed in the previous market period. Usually applied to farm commodities, it explains the wide fluctuations in price and output which may occur in agricultural markets.

Common Agricultural Policy (CAP). The system of intervention in agricultural markets within the EC designed to maintain farm incomes and encourage output. 'Intervention prices' are maintained by the commission for each commodity by buying and storing surplus production.

Complementary Goods. Goods are complementary when a reduction in the price of one of the goods results in an increased demand for both goods, for example a reduction in the price of cars increases the demand for both cars and petrol.

Consumer Surplus. The surplus of utility which consumers receive resulting from the difference between the market price they actually pay for a good and what they would be prepared to pay rather than go without it.

Consumption Function. The relationship between aggregate consumption expenditure and aggregate disposable income in an economy. A central feature of the Keynesian model, in which consumption is assumed to be a function of income.

Consumption Goods. Goods purchased by consumers for final consumption rather than for the production of further goods. May be single use, e.g. ice-cream or durable, e.g. refrigerators.

Contestable Markets. Oligopolistic markets where the barriers to entry are low hence the threat of potential entry modifies the behaviour of the firms in that market. A perfectly contestable market is one without sunk cost, making entry easier.

Corporation Tax. A tax on the profits of companies.

Cost-push Inflation. Inflation which arises from increased cost factors such as the price of materials or labour. It is independent of the level of demand.

Currency Appreciation. An increase in the exchange rate of one currency relative to others in a regime of flexible exchange rates. In a fixed exchange rate system referred to as revaluation.

Currency Depreciation. A fall in the exchange rate of one currency relative to others in a regime of flexible exchange rates. In a fixed exchange rate system referred to as devaluation.

Cyclical Unemployment. Unemployment which results from the downward fluctuations in the trade cycle.

Death Rate (Crude). The number of deaths occurring in any year for every 1000 of the population.

Deflation. A reduction in the general level of prices brought about by monetary and fiscal policies designed to reduce the level of economic activity.

Demand. The desire and ability of consumers to purchase an amount of a particular good or service.

Demand Curve. A curve which relates the prices of a commodity to the quantity the consumer is willing to purchase. Conventionally price is shown on the Y axis and quantity on the X axis. The demand curve slopes downward from left to right reflecting the 'law of downward sloping demand '.

Demand-pull Inflation. Inflation which results from aggregate demand in the economy exceeding the full employment output of goods and services. If aggregate demand exceeds aggregate supply prices will rise, if these price rises are sustained the result is inflation.

Demand Shift. An increase or decrease in the quantity demanded at each price as a consequence of a change in factors other than price e.g. taste, preferences, incomes. Represented by a shift in the entire demand curve upwards to the right in the case of an increase, and downwards to the left in the case of a decrease.

Depression. A severe downturn in the trade cycle characterised by high levels of unemployment, in particular the UK 1929 - 1933.

Developing Country. A country with a low level of GNP per head, which has not reached the stage of industrialisation.

Development Areas. Those areas in the UK which because of their high levels of unemployment are deemed by the government as qualifying for special assistance e.g. development grants.

Discount Market. Also referred to as the money market, consists of the banks, discount houses, and accepting houses. The market deals in Treasury bills, bills of exchange, and short dated bonds. It is important to the authorities for its role as an intermediary between the Bank of England and the banking system.

Diseconomy. The long-run tendency for average cost of production to rise after reaching a minimum point. Generally due to problems of administration and co-ordination.

Disposable Income. Personal income, after the deduction of taxation and receipt of benefits, available for spending or saving.

Division of Labour. The breaking down of a task into its simplest components in order to facilitate specialisation of labour and/or mechanisation. The basis of surplus production and the exchange economy.

Dumping. The sale of excess production at the marginal cost of production in export markets in order to increase profits in the domestic market or to eliminate competition.

Durable Goods (Consumer). Consumer goods such as refrigerators which are not consumed immediately but over a period of time. More accurately it is the service or utility which they yield which is consumed.

Economic Growth. Refers to growth of national income which is generally taken to imply rising living standards.

Economic Rent. The return to a factor in fixed supply which is considered to be a surplus the size of which is determined by the price of the factor. Where there are transfer earnings it is the surplus payments over the transfer earrings.

Economies of Scale. As the scale of production increases with successive increases in plant size there is a tendency for average costs per unit of output to decline due to the economies of large scale production.

Elasticity of Demand (Price). The degree of responsiveness of quantity demanded to changes in price. In response to a price change therefore total revenue may increase, stay unchanged or fall. Measured by the formula

$$PED = \frac{\text{percentage change in quantity demanded}}{\text{percentage change in price}}$$

The resulting coefficient of elasticity will be, < 1 (inelastic), = 1 (Unitary), or > 1 (Elastic).

Elasticity of Supply (Price). The degree of responsiveness of quantity supplied to changes in price. The coefficient of elasticity of supply is measured as:

$$PES = \frac{\text{percentage change in quantity supplied}}{\text{percentage change in price}}$$

Entrepreneur. The name given to an individual in economics who manages and owns his own business, thereby providing the capital and enterprise, accepting all the risks, and receiving all the profit as a reward.

Equilibrium. An important concept in economics referring to a situation where opposing forces are in balance and there is no further tendency to change. In a market equilibrium would exist when the quantities demanded by consumers was exactly equal to the quantity supplied by producers at the prevailing price.

European Monetary System (EMS). An attempt by the EU to establish a system which would keep the fluctuations between the currencies of the member countries within narrow bands.

European Union (EU). Established by the Treaty of Rome in 1957 for the purposes of creating a customs union. The objective of the treaty was to eliminate obstacles to the free movement of goods, labour and capital between the member countries; to establish an external tariff, and a common agricultural policy (CAP). The basic idea is to form a large trading bloc to compete with other large blocs such as the USA and USSR. The original 6 member countries had grown to 13 by 1987.

Exchange Rate. The price of a currency expressed in terms of another currency, which is also the rate at which the currencies can be exchanged.

Excise Duties. Taxes levied upon goods for domestic consumption.

Externalities. An externality exists when the production or consumption of a good by one party imposes costs or benefits upon another party, but will not be included in the decisions of the party creating them.

Factors of Production. The essential requirements necessary for production to occur, namely, land, labour, and capital. These are combined by enterprise to produce economic goods.

Fiduciary Issue. Paper money not backed by gold. The fiduciary issue is backed only by confidence in the currency unit. The note issue is now entirely fiduciary.

Fixed costs. Those costs of production which in the short run do not change with output, e.g. rent, rates, interest.

Fixed Exchange Rates. A system whereby a group of trading nations agrees to maintain a par value for their own currency relative to the others through intervention on the foreign exchange markets. Such a system was operated by the IMF members from 1947 to 1973.

Flexible Exchange Rates. A system whereby the rate of exchange is determined by the market forces of supply and demand.

Frictional Unemployment. Unemployment which results from the time lag between labour becoming unemployed and locating a suitable vacancy. It may exist therefore during periods of high employment and can be a consequence of job changing.

Friedman, Milton. Professor of Economics at Chicago University and a leading exponent of monetarism.

Full Employment. In terms of gross domestic product it is a measure of the output which the economy is capable of when all its resources are employed. For labour it is taken to mean that everyone who desires a job at the current wage rate is employed and only frictional unemployment remains.

Funding Operations. The process of changing the structure of the national debt by converting short term debt to long term debt.

General Agreement on Tariffs and Trade (GATT). Established in 1948 with the objective of reducing tariffs and other barriers to trade, and to encourage free-trade between the 88 members. Replaced by the World Trade Organisation in 1995.

Gilt-edged Securities. British government securities with fixed rates of interest, traded on the Stock Exchange.

Gold and Foreign Exchange Reserves. Stock of gold and foreign currency held by a nation for the settlement of international indebtedness if required to do so.

Gross Domestic Product (GDP). The total output of goods and services produced by the economy over a year, expressed as a monetary value.

Gross National Product (GNP). Gross domestic product plus income earned from overseas investment owned by UK residents less income paid abroad to foreign residents.

Horizontal Integration. The merging of different firms at the same stage in the manufacturing process.

Import Duties. Taxes imposed on imported goods. May be ad valorem (according to value) or specific (per unit).

Import Quotas. A form of import control whereby only certain quantities of specified goods may be imported.

Imports. The goods and services which enter a country from overseas sources for domestic consumption.

Income Tax. A tax on incomes. In the UK deducted by employers at source and paid to the Inland Revenue; referred to as Pay-as-You-Earn income tax (PAYE).

Incremental Capital-Output Ratio (ICOR). The ratio of net investment to the change in output over a given period, i.e. the additional output gained from new investment.

Inflation. A generalised and sustained rise in the price level or a fall in the value of money.

Inflationary Gap. The excess of aggregate monetary demand over aggregate supply measured at the full employment level of national income.

Interest. The reward for foregoing current consumption.

Interest, Rate of. The price of borrowed money. The price a borrower must pay a lender to compensate for foregone consumption.

International Bank for Reconstruction and Development (IBRD). Known also as the 'World Bank'. Established at the Bretton Woods Conference 1944 with the purpose of encouraging capital investment for the reconstruction and development of its member countries either by making loans from its own funds or by the direction of private funds to suitable projects.

International Monetary Fund (IMF). Established at the Bretton Woods Conference 1944 and effective from 1947. The purpose of the fund was to encourage international co-operation on trade and payments. Was responsible for the management of the fixed exchange rate system which operated from 1947 to 1973, and provided a fund to assist member nations with temporary balance of payments difficulties.

Investment. Expenditure on capital goods.

J-Curve. Name given to the observation that following a currency depreciation the balance of payments generally deteriorates before eventually improving. If graphed the trend looks like a letter J.

Keynes, John Maynard (1883-1946). Author of *'The General Theory of Employment, Interest, and Money'* (1936). His writings formed the basis of the post-war economic policies of demand management, i.e. The 'Keynesian Model' in which governments utilise their own expenditure in order to manage the level of demand.

Kondratieff Cycle. After the economist M.D. Kondratieff, the proposal that there are long term cycles in the trade cycle with peaks and troughs every 50-60 years.

Laffer Curve. After Professor Arthur Laffer, a curve relating tax revenue to the tax rate.

Lean Production. The removal of all non value adding activities from manufacturing process from the suppliers to the final customer. The focus of operation is on core, or value adding, activities. Includes the elimination of waste through rigorous control of quality and inventory.

Lender of Last Resort. An essential feature of the role of a central bank is the provision of a facility for loans to the banking system when required to do so, in the UK through the medium of the discount market. This lending is done on the central bank's own terms which enable it to influence the general level of interest rates and the money supply.

Liquidity. The ease with which an asset can be converted into money.

Liquidity Preference. The extent to which individuals desire to hold their wealth in the form of money rather than other assets such as bonds.

Long-run. The period of time in which the firm can adjust all its factors of production, both variable and fixed.

Macroeconomics. The study of the aggregate performance of the whole of gross national product and the price level.

Marginal Cost. The additional cost resulting from a small (or single unit) increase in the output of a good.

Marginal Product. The increase in total output resulting from a small increase in one factor of production whilst all the other factors are held constant. Can be applied to labour, land, or capital i.e. marginal productivity of labour etc.

Marginal Propensity to Consume (MPC). The proportion of each additional unit of income which is devoted to consumption. As not all income is normally consumed the value of the MPC is usually less than one. The size of the MPC determines the slope of the consumption function and plays an important part in the multiplier process.

Marginal Propensity to Save (MPS). The proportion of each additional unit of income which is devoted to saving. As income is either consumed or saved it has a value of 1 - MPC.

Marginal Revenue. The change in a firm's total revenue which results from the sale of one additional unit of output.

Marginal Utility. The increase in total utility gained by increasing the quantity consumed of a good by one unit.

Marginal Utility, Law of Diminishing. As successive units of a good are consumed the extra utility received from each additional unit tends to diminish. Underlies the theory of demand.

Microeconomics. The study of individual economic units, consumers and firms and the ways in which they make their decisions. The central concept is the role of the market.

Minimum Lending Rate (MLR). The rate of interest at which the central bank is prepared to lend to the banking system in its role as 'lender of the last resort'.

Monetarism. The school of macroeconomic thought that suggests that the money supply is the most important factor in determining the level of expenditure and prices.

Money. Anything which is generally accepted in exchange for goods, or in settlement of a debt.

Money Supply. The quantity of money which exists in an economy at any single time. As there is no single definition of money different definitions may be utilised for operational purposes such as M0, M4 etc.

Monopoly. A market in which a single seller controls the entire output of a good or service.

Multiplier (The). A measure of the effect on national income of a change in one of the components of aggregate demand. A central element in the Keynesian model of demand management, generally referred to in terms of investment or government expenditure.

Calculated as:–

$$\frac{1}{1 - MPC}$$

where MPC = marginal propensity to consume.

National Debt. The cumulative total of outstanding debts owed by successive governments

National Income. The aggregate or total income of the nation which results from economic activity, measured in monetary terms, over a specified time period - usually a year.

Net Investment. Gross expenditure on capital formation less investment to replace worn out plant and equipment

Oligopoly. A market which is dominated by a few large sellers i.e. there is a high degree of concentration in the market.

Open Market Operations. The purchase and sale of securities by the central bank on the open market in order to influence the stock of financial assets and thereby indirectly the lending of the banks.

Opportunity Cost. Cost defined in terms of the value of the alternatives which have been foregone in order to achieve a particular objective.

Optimum. The best outcome which can be achieved from a given set of variables.

Organisation of Economic Co-operation and Development (OECD). Established in 1961, the organisation's aims are the encouragement of economic growth and high employment among the member countries, to assist in the economic development of the less advanced member and non member countries, and the expansion of multilateral world trade. The organisation functions through a number of committees and publishes a regular statistical bulletin.

Organisation Of Petroleum Exporting Countries (OPEC). A group of fourteen countries who are the major producers and exporters of crude oil. Established in 1960, it attempts to fix prices and production quotas for crude oil exports.

Participation Rate. The proportion of the population who are of working age and are part of the labour force.

Per capita income. Income per head of population. i.e.

$$\frac{NY}{population}$$

Phillips Curve. The empirical proposition put forward by Professor A.W. Phillips in 1958 that there was a significant inverse relationship between the level of unemployment and the rate of change of money wages.

Precautionary Motive. Money held for the purpose of meeting unforeseen expenditures.

Prices and Incomes Policy. Government policy aimed at regulating the rate of increase of wages and prices in order to control inflation.

Principal-Agent Problem. A feature of asymmetric information resulting in the problem of resource allocation which arises from the difficulty of imposing contracts forcing agents to act in their principals best interests.

Privatisation. The sale of government holdings in nationalised industries to the private sector.

Productivity. The rate at which output flows from the use of factors of production. Often used in terms of productivity to mean efficiency.

Public Sector Borrowing Requirement (PSBR). The deficit between the income and expenditure of the public sector, in particular central and local government. Usually financed by debt sales to the 'non bank' private sector, borrowing from the banking system, borrowing from overseas, or by issuing more cash to the public.

Quantity Theory of Money. A theory of the relationship between the supply of money in an economy and the price level.

Rate of Return. Net profit as a percentage of capital employed in a business. An important measure of business efficiency.

Real Income. Income measured in terms of the goods and services it will actually purchase.

Real Wages. Money wages deflated by an index such as the retail price index to give the actual purchasing power implied.

Reflation. Policy measures designed to raise the level of aggregate demand closer to the full employment level of national income.

Rent–see Economic Rent

Retail Price Index. An index used to express current retail prices in terms of a base year. The index is based on a weighted average of typical consumer expenditure patterns.

Saving. Desisting from using income for current consumption, as income which is not consumed must be saved. Note that this is not investment, it only becomes investment when the saved funds are used to acquire an asset.

Seasonal Unemployment. Unemployment which arises from the seasonal nature of some types of work such as the holiday related industries.

Short-Run. The time period during which the firm can adjust only its variable factors of production, such as labour.

Social Cost. Occur when actions by one party create costs which are borne by others or by society as a whole.

Special Deposits. Cash deposits by the clearing banks with the Bank of England in response to a directive by the Bank in order to restrict credit creation.

Special Drawing Rights (SDRs). Used by the IMF to finance international trade. Countries with balance of payments difficulties could draw up to 125% of the quota they contributed to the fund, but with increasingly severe conditions regarding their domestic economic policies imposed upon them.

Speculative Motive. Money balances held for the purposes of avoiding losses on a declining securities market. An innovation to monetary theory by J.M. Keynes to explain liquidity preference.

Structural Unemployment. Arises out of fundamental changes in the industrial base of the economy. Generally associated with the decline of 'staple' industries concentrated in the regions, hence also related to the 'regional problem'.

Supply. The quantity of goods or services which a producer is willing to put on to the market at the prevailing price during a particular time period.

Supply Curve. A curve illustrating the relationship between the market price of a good and the quantity supplied. The convention is that price is shown on the Y axis and quantity on the X axis. Supply curves generally slope upwards to the right.

Supply-Side Economies. A view of macroeconomics which emerged during the 1970s but with much in common with the classical tradition of economics. Supply-side economists take the view that output is determined by real variables and therefore stress the importance of the growth of the supply of the factors of production and technological change. They also suggest that fiscal and monetary policy cannot influence real output in the long run.

Tariff–see Import duties

Terms of Trade. The ratio of the index of export prices to the index of import prices. If export prices rise more quickly than import prices the index rises and represents an improvement in the terms of trade and vice versa.

Trade Barrier. A term used to describe any restriction on international trade imposed by government.

Transactions Demand for Money. The demand for cash balances to finance normal expenditures between receipts of income.

Transfer Earnings. The returns to a factor of production which are just sufficient to keep it in its current use. Any excess over transfer earnings is economic rent.

Transfer payments. Income transfers between different groups in society. For example from the employed to the unemployed, or students in the form of grants. Deliberately excluded from national income calculations as to include them would result in 'double counting'.

Treasury Bills. One of the means by which the government covers its short term borrowing requirement. The bills have a maturity of 91 days after which they are redeemable with interest. The amounts vary between £5000 and £1 million and are issued by tender to the money market.

Unemployment, Natural Rate of. The unemployment which remains when the labour market is in equilibrium. Such unemployment is therefore considered voluntary in the sense that the unemployed labour is not willing to work for a sufficiently low wage. Associated with the monetarist view.

Utility. The satisfaction derived from the consumption of a good or service.

Value Judgement. A statement of opinion which cannot be validated by appeal to the facts.

Vertical Integration. The merging of firms at different stages of the production process, either backwards towards the source of raw materials or forwards towards the retail stage.

World Trade Organisation. Established to monitor world trade and encourage free trade. Set up in 1995 to replace GATT.

Yield. The income from a security as a percentage of its current market price.

Index